PANACHE **DIRECTORY**
phoenix

PROFESSIONALS, PRODUCTS AND SERVICES

INTERIOR DESIGN

Judy Fox Interiors
4147 N Goldwater Blvd, Suite 101
Scottsdale, AZ 85251
(480) 860-6475
jFoxjfi@aol.com
www.judyfoxinteriors.com

CABINETRY

Kitchens Southwest
15685 N Greenway-Hayden Loop,
Suite 300
Scottsdale, AZ 85260
(480) 443-0102
dhayes@kitchenssouthwest.com
www.kitchenssouthwest.com

OUTDOOR KITCHENS AND FIREPLACES

Sub Zero - Wolf
15570 North 83rd Way
Scottsdale, AZ 85260
(480) 921-0900
showroom@subzerowolfsouthwest.com
www.subzero.com/phoenix

PANACHE DIRECTORY is an exclusive collection of elite professionals recommended as the best-of-the-best by their clients and peers. Selected for their outstanding craftsmanship and unbeatable service, these professionals have a reputation for setting the bar in their respective trades and delivering exceptional quality in every detail of every job.

Overland Gallery of Fine Art
Art Galleries

APPLIANCES

Sub Zero - Wolf
15570 North 83rd Way
Scottsdale, AZ 85260
(480) 921-0900
showroom@subzerowolfsouthwest.com
www.subzero.com/phoenix

ART GALLERIES

Overland Gallery of Fine Art
7155 Main Street
Scottsdale, AZ 85251
(480) 947-1934
Trudy@OverlandGallery.com
www.overlandgallery.com

S.R. Brennen Gallery
7150 E. Main St.
Scottsdale, AZ 85251
(480) 994-1355
Art@SRBrennenGallery.com
www.SRBrennengalleries.com

AUDIO-VISUAL

Active Security and Sound Services
Russell Bickle
6907 E. Minton Street
Mesa, AZ 85207
(480) 659-1406
ActiveSecurity@hotmail.com
www.ActiveSecurityandSound.com

CATERING

Ciao Baby Catering
21 E 6th Street, Suite 114
Tempe, AZ 85281
(480) 257-2426
www.ciaobabycatering.com

CABINETRY

Kitchens Southwest
15685 N Greenway-Hayden Loop, Suite 300
Scottsdale, AZ 85260
(480) 443-0102
dhayes@kitchenssouthwest.com
www.kitchenssouthwest.com

CUSTOM FURNITURE

Feathers Custom Furniture
Dan and Claudia Levinson
15330 N. Hayden Road, Suite 110
Scottsdale, AZ 85260
(480) 905-1396
Claudia@feathersdesign.com
www.feathersdesign.com

Feathers Custom Furnishings
Furniture

DENTISTRY

Healthy Smiles Dentistry
9787 North 91st Street, Suite 102
Scottsdale, AZ 85258
(480) 951-0651
schwartzdds@aol.com
www.healthysmilesdentistry.com

DRAPERIES AND WINDOW TREATMENTS

Brandt's Interiors
Karen Bierk
4848 E. Cactus Road
Scottsdale, AZ 85254
(602) 996-3040
brandtsinteriors@aol.com
wwww.brandts2.com

FRAMING AND ART

Think Art
15125 N. Hayden Road, Suite 101
Scottsdale, AZ 85260
(480) 998-9790
www.ThinkFineArt.com

FURNITURE

Bungalow
15330 North Hayden Road, Suite 120
Scottsdale, AZ 85260
(480) 948-5409
alicia@bungalowaz.com
www.bungalowaz.com

One Posh Place
Paige Bailey, Owner/Interior Designer
5625 E. Indian School Road
Phoenix, AZ 85018
(480) 941-8954
Oneposhplace@gmail.com
www.oneposhplaceaz.com

HARDWOOD FLOORING & REFINISHING

Enmar Hardwood Flooring, Inc.
560 E. Germann, Suite 105
Gilbert, AZ 85297
(480) 497-1633
Tricia@enmarflooring.com
www.EnmarFlooring.com

HANDYMAN SERVICES

Handyman Connection
11435 N. Cave Creek Road, Suite 202
Phoenix, AZ 85020
(602) 424-6700
http://phoenix.handymanconnection.com

Visit **WWW.PANACHEDIRECTORY.COM** to view more
information on these elite, talented professionals

NTRAL PARK Tribeca
Broadway

Bungalow
Furniture

LOUIS VUITTON

Linen Tree
Home Decor

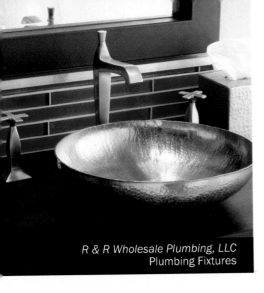

R & R Wholesale Plumbing, LLC
Plumbing Fixtures

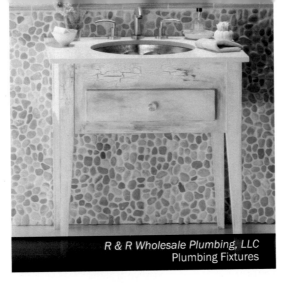

R & R Wholesale Plumbing, LLC
Plumbing Fixtures

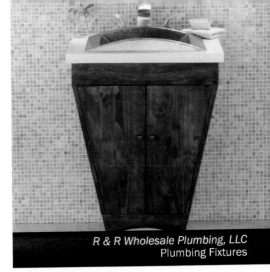

R & R Wholesale Plumbing, LLC
Plumbing Fixtures

HOME DECOR

The Linen Tree
6137 N. Scottsdale Road, Suite 111
Scottsdale, AZ 85250
(480) 483-2044
info@thelinentree.com
www.thelinentree.com

INTERIOR DESIGN

C. Stark Design Inc.
Cathy Stark
5922 Evening Night Glow Circle
Scottsdale, AZ 85266
(480) 563-9336
cstarkdesign@gmail.com
www.cstarkdesign.com

Chesterfield's Design, SW
Kay Schulz, Interior Designer
12578 East Saddlehorn Trail
Scottsdale, AZ 85259
(480) 314-7712
chesterfieldsdesign@gmail.com
www.ChesterfieldsDesign.com

Kimberly Colletti
Treken Interiors
8265 East Del Cadena Drive
Scottsdale, AZ 85258
(480) 596-9500
Kimberly@TrekenInteriors.com
www.TrekenInteriors.com

KITCHEN DESIGN AND REMODELING

One Posh Place
Paige Bailey, Owner/Interior Designer
5625 E. Indian School Road
Phoenix, AZ 85018
(480) 941-8954
Oneposhplace@gmail.com
www.oneposhplaceaz.com

MOVING SERVICES

Fully Loaded Deliveries
Chris Berg
2640 E. Rose Garden, Suite 3
Phoenix, AZ 85050
(480) 307-8077
Chris@FullyLoadedDeliveries.com
www.FullyLoadedDeliveries.com

OUTDOOR KITCHENS AND FIREPLACES

Sub Zero - Wolf
15570 North 83rd Way
Scottsdale, AZ 85260
(480) 921-0900
showroom@subzerowolfsouthwest.com
www.subzero.com/phoenix

PEST CONTROL

Eco-Logic Management, Inc.
Michael Neal, Owner
Frank Abbaete, Owner
Cave Creek, AZ 85331
(602) 585-8485
MnEcoLogic@yahoo.com

Kitchens Southwest
Kitchen Design and Remodeling

PLUMBING FIXTURES

R & R Wholesale Plumbing, LLC
7830 E. Redfield Road, Suite 8
Scottsdale, AZ 85260
(480) 991-9624
BrianT88@gmail.com
www.rrwholesale.net

PLUMBING SERVICE
AND CONSTRUCTION

Younger Brothers Plumbing
8525 North 75th Avenue
Peoria, AZ 85345
(623) 487-3300
customerservice@ybcco.com
www.ybcco.com

POOL/BILLIARDS
AND GAME TABLES

Diamondback Billiards & Games - Glendale
6027 West Bell Road, Suite B
Glendale, AZ 85308
(602) 843-1320
rusty@diamondbackbilliards.com
www.diamondbackbilliards.com

Diamondback Billiards & Games - Mesa
2534 West Broadway Road, Suite 6
Mesa, AZ 85202
(480) 967-7755
rusty@diamondbackbilliards.com
www.diamondbackbilliards.com

SECURITY
ALARM SYSTEMS

Active Security and Sound Services
Russell Bickle
6907 E. Minton Street
Mesa, AZ 85207
(480) 659-1406
ActiveSecurity@hotmail.com
www.ActiveSecurityandSound.com

TERMITE SERVICES

Eco-Logic Management, Inc.
Michael Neal, Owner
Frank Abbaete, Owner
Cave Creek, AZ 85331
(602) 585-8485
MnEcoLogic@yahoo.com

WINDOW TREATMENTS
AND DRAPERIES

Blind Devotion
Jerry Levinson
1986 North Alma School Road
Chandler, AZ 85224
(480) 917-2707
www.BlindDevotion.com

Mr. P's Blind & Shade Co.
Eric Auffant
7689 East Paradise Lane, Suite 2
Scottsdale, AZ 85260
(480) 947-1854
Eric@mrps.com
www.mrps.com

S.R. Brennen Gallery
Art Galleries

Diamondback Billiards 7 Games
Pool/Billiards and Game Tables

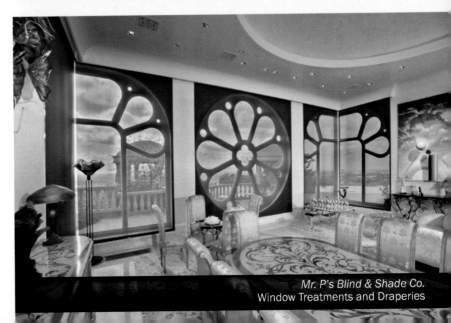

Mr. P's Blind & Shade Co.
Window Treatments and Draperies

perspectives
ON DESIGN
southwest

design philosophies expressed by the southwest's leading professionals

Published by

PANACHE
PANACHE PARTNERS

Panache Partners, LLC
1424 Gables Court
Plano, TX 75075
469.246.6060
Fax: 469.246.6062
www.panache.com

Publishers: Brian G. Carabet and John A. Shand
Executive Publisher: Phil Reavis
Senior Associate Publisher: Karla Setser
Associate Publisher: Vicki Beaudoin
Director of Development & Design: Beth Benton Buckley
Publication & Circulation Manager: Lauren Castelli
Senior Designer: Emily A. Kattan
Editor: Anita M. Kasmar
Managing Production Coordinator: Kristy Randall

Printed in Malaysia

Distributed by Independent Publishers Group
800.888.4741

PUBLISHER'S DATA

Perspectives on Design Southwest

Library of Congress Control Number: 2009933252

ISBN 13: 978-1-933415-83-3
ISBN 10: 1-933415-83-5

First Printing 2010

10 9 8 7 6 5 4 3 2 1

Previous Page: Shiflet Group Architects, page 49

This publication is intended to showcase the work of extremely talented
people. The publisher does not require, warrant, endorse or verify any
professional accreditations, educational backgrounds or professional
affiliations of the individuals or firms included herein. All copy and
photography published herein has been reviewed and approved as free
of any usage fees or rights and accurate by the individuals and/or firms
included herein.

Panache Partners, LLC, is dedicated to the restoration and conservation
of the environment. Our books are manufactured using paper from
mills certified to derive their products from well-managed forests. We
are committed to continued investigation of alternative paper products
and environmentally responsible manufacturing processes to ensure the
preservation of our fragile planet.

Bentwood Luxury Kitchens, page 145

Peterson Architecture & Associates, page 29

La Scimmia Studios, page 251

Schenck & Company, page 163

Picasso Tile & Design, page 131

Desert Star Construction, page 67

Russ Berger Design Group, page 197

Judy Fox Interiors, page 213

Paul J. Labadie Craftsman Company, page 157

Palmer Todd, page 193

Bell-Borja Studios, page 231

introduction

Creating the spaces in which we live and achieving the beauty we desire can be a daunting quest—a quest that is as diverse as each of our unique personalities. For some, it may be serene hardscaped gardens; for others it may be opulent marble entryways. Aspiring chefs may find a kitchen boasting the finest in technology their true sanctuary.

Perspectives on Design Southwest is a pictorial journey from conceptualizing your dream home to putting together the finishing touches to creating an outdoor oasis. Alongside the phenomenal photography, you will have a rare insight to how these tastemakers achieve such works of art and be inspired by their personal perspectives on design.

Within these pages, the region's finest artisans will share their wisdom, experience and talent. It is the collaboration between these visionaries and the outstanding pride and craftsmanship of the products showcased that together achieve the remarkable. Learn from leaders in the industry about the aesthetics of a finely crafted sofa, how appropriate lighting can dramatically change the appearance of a room and what is necessary to create a state-of-the-art home theater.

Whether your dream is to have a new home or one that has been redesigned to suit your lifestyle, *Perspectives on Design Southwest* will be both an enjoyable journey and a source of motivation.

Pool-Quest, page 315

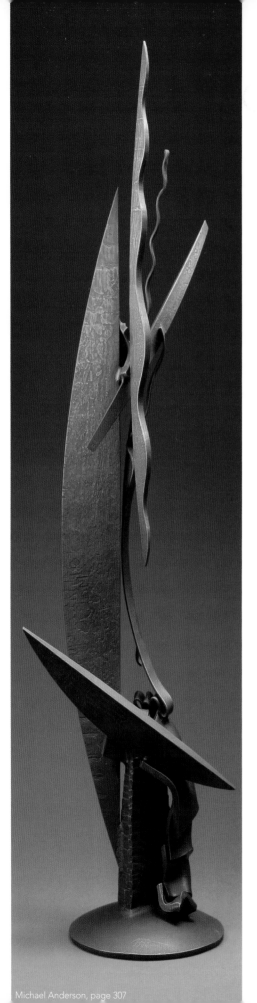

chapter one: the concept

chapter two: the structure

chapter three: elements of structure

contents

chapter four: elements of design

chapter five: living the elements

Shiflet Group Architects, page 49

Pinnacle Architectural Studio, page 39

the concept

chapter one

Fascinated with buildings since the age of five, Robert Bacon proudly designed his first custom home and saw it built while he was still in high school. Bob's ambitions were realized early, and his body of experience grew rapidly as he became involved in virtually all areas of the built environment soon after studying architecture at Arizona State University.

Bob's zest for learning and passion for architecture are evident in all of his creations. "I enjoy the fact that creating the built environment can involve every aspect of human knowledge and experience," says Bob. His holistic approach considers the site's climate, terrain and natural features as well as the region's cultural heritage. Bob has founded several entrepreneurial businesses, each of which focused on a unique niche in the design-building industry—from energy management to hospitality, luxury residential and commercial design. Today he is the president of Bacon Ventures and The Bacon Collections, with offices in Arizona and New Hampshire. These innovative consulting and design firms are renowned for community planning and environmental design as well as for pioneering work in information management and custom-quality, predesigned home packages that serve builders, custom lot developers and end-user clients throughout the United States.

"An important goal of desert work is to capture the powerful beauty of the landscape by integrating the home with its surroundings."

—Bob Bacon

THE BACON COLLECTIONS

"The greatest inspirations of many projects are the site, the surrounding geography and the region's cultural influences."

—Bob Bacon

RIGHT: The primary views from the two-story home face west toward the city lights and spectacular desert sunsets. We designed this luxurious Arizona ranch with large overhangs covering truly functional outdoor living spaces that are ideal for entertaining as they allow a seamless flow of space and circulation from indoors to out.

PREVIOUS PAGES: The predominantly horizontal home hugs its site near the prow of a hill and incorporates extensive glass and broad overhangs to frame panoramic views of the Valley of the Sun below. Its desert material and color palette includes weathered copper fascias and the blue-grey hue of Pennsylvania bluestone while the interior is finely detailed with the warmth of clear redwood and complemented with cherry wood and black accents. The home nestles into its prominent setting and responds to the desert environment with an exquisitely proportioned arrangement of architectural and landscape elements.

Photographs by Dino Tonn Photography

"At their best, well-designed environments evoke deep emotional responses that transcend style and fashion."

—Bob Bacon

ABOVE: Overlooking the Valley of the Sun below, the south-facing façade incorporates deep overhangs and long horizontal lines interrupted by vertical elements that visually anchor the structure to the site.

FACING PAGE: The gallery hall showcases ancient Chinese artifacts in a quiet and elegantly detailed space where cherry wood doors, floors and mouldings are complemented by custom carpet runners and black absolute granite steps that create a simple, yet graceful, palette of materials and colors. The design exercises restraint in its careful use of color, pattern and texture to achieve a well-balanced composition that carefully attends to every detail.
Photographs by Dino Tonn Photography

ABOVE & FACING PAGE: We design indoor-outdoor environments that allow for the best in regional living. By bringing together creative designers and expert craftsmen, we create total living environments that are both practical and beautiful, dissolving the boundaries between indoors and out and enabling comfortable and convenient outdoor living any time of the day, any day of the year.

Photographs by Dino Tonn Photography

"In visually fragile environments such as southwestern deserts, it is imperative to achieve a minimal visual impact on the site's inherent beauty by reflecting the colors, textures, massing and scale of the natural setting."

—Bob Bacon

ABOVE: The two-story desert contemporary design achieves a one-story appearance with its low profile and predominantly horizontal profile. The living areas are extended into the landscape by patios that feature an outdoor kitchen, dramatic fire feature, water-wall and swimming pool to accommodate year-round entertaining.

FACING PAGE: The home's careful arrangement of windows and overhangs frames the panoramic views of the Phoenix area, including a spectacular view of Camelback Mountain and the "Praying Monk" toward the east. The texture and pattern of the Pennsylvania bluestone lends counterpoint to the natural warmth and elegant qualities of the cherry and redwood used throughout the home. The balance of elegant detailing and bold forms creates a timeless sense of refinement that is matched by an enduring sense of strength and durability. All vestiges of modern technology, such as televisions and air conditioning outlets, have been carefully integrated or discreetly hidden so as not to detract from the art of the architecture and its contents.
Photographs by Dino Tonn Photography

After more than 30 years in residential architecture, Mark Candelaria is excited about the future—and so are his clients. Mark recognizes that too often homeowners have a sense of urgency to complete their homes, and with this outlook, a home's design can suffer. By taking each facet of the design process with great care and thought, Mark collaborates with his clients to draw out the functionality and distinct elements that each space requires; an extra month or two in the design process is well worth the end result. Mark insists that no matter the home's style, restraint is key. A home should never be a hodge-podge of styles but rather a distinctive, timeless expression. By working with his clients' mission statement—procured through a series of questions, magazine clippings, home tours and frequent dialogue—Mark can distill and guide the project's direction.

Lifestyle comes before style in a Candelaria Design home. A house set in its proper context that captures views, prevailing breezes and, most importantly, the homeowners' personality will always result in a place that clients are proud to call their own.

"People who give their house a life allow it, in return, to become a part of theirs."

—Mark Candelaria

CANDELARIA DESIGN

"When homeowners are in the process of remodeling, their tendency is to add endless ornate architectural features. But actually, it is within a refined simplicity that homes are improved and remain timeless."

—Mark Candelaria

RIGHT: One of the first things that stood out to me about my clients' 1980s-built house was the porte-cochère. They wanted a substantial remodeling, and my top priority was to show them how the entry could be improved if the porte-cochère were removed. When I sketched the space without the ornate covered entry, the homeowners were astounded at how less actually is more in some cases.
Photograph by Jim Christy

PREVIOUS PAGES LEFT: We've often felt that homeowners in general have forgotten about their front yard and what a great space it can be for socializing with neighbors. Within the context of the neighborhood, we incorporated an outdoor living area around a fire pit. Not only can the homeowners watch their kids play, but evening barbecues are easily facilitated. The outdoor living area also blends well with the cottage-type ambience the owners requested—dormer windows and brick accents keep the language simple.
Photograph by Christiaan Blok

PREVIOUS PAGES RIGHT: In response to our clients' request for a formal façade to make a strong statement, we worked with a symmetrical layout that revolved around the central axis of the house. Always aware of the functionality requirements, we took note that the family had five children, three boys and two girls, and placed their bedrooms in special wings of the house. What makes the home so successful is the delicate balance of formal yet inviting spaces for every member of the family. Defining the elegant arrival to the house is a faux limestone entry surround, which we designed using precast concrete that was aged to look like limestone, set behind an antique limestone fountain. Among the home's fun and laid-back features is a pool cabana.
Photograph by Christiaan Blok

"You can't just walk in and start tearing things apart. With every home there is a step-by-step educational process in which a complete vision must be articulated before construction can begin."

—Mark Candelaria

ABOVE: A good friend of mine bought a ranch home that was defined by very strong Asian characteristics, but we really didn't feel that it reflected his personality. After stripping some of the surfaces, we discovered an amazing terracotta floor and wood beams that were actually stunningly warm without the flaky white paint. We unified the inside and outside by adding large pocket doors and windows, and we even had a bit of humor emerge with the homeowner's Andy Warhol painting of Howdy Doody.

FACING PAGE: It's always an enjoyable challenge to work with a couple who's getting married and trying to merge their individual styles. Because a bachelor pad was nowhere near conducive to two new family members, we knew that it needed more space and also a warmer, family-friendly ambience. Its Santa Fe style incorporates a second-floor trellis, an enclosed garage and a handful of tiny outdoor living spaces.
Photographs by Christiaan Blok

"Bedrooms are essentially just big boxes with a few windows, but kitchens and bathrooms are my favorite—from construction to equipment and lighting, there's the whole gamut right in one very active area of the house."

—Mark Candelaria

ABOVE LEFT: A mountain home in Flagstaff needed to facilitate the homeowner's love for cooking and traveling. Because of the mountainous atmosphere, we wanted an earthy feel that embodied a level of sophistication. Its rustic ambience is perfectly complemented by a commercial-grade range.
Photograph by Alexander Vertikoff

ABOVE RIGHT: The character and detailing of a north Scottsdale kitchen were completely different. We wanted to capture a celebration of space, and the brick ceiling helps bring a cozy facet. The island is made of mesquite wood in a checkerboard pattern and works well with the ceiling to help neutralize the height and grandeur of the space.
Photograph by Tim Matthewson, Candelaria Design

FACING PAGE: Working with an inner-city home prompted us to create views within the living space. To give it a luscious resort feel, we designed a beautiful cabana. An arcade wall connects the indoor and outdoor spaces the entire length of the home and creates a unique interplay with this self-created backyard.
Photograph by Christiaan Blok

"Some houses are renovated on a predictable rotation, but those that are developed properly, slowly over time, are the ones that last."

—Mark Candelaria

ABOVE: "Let's create an Italian hill town on the mountain." That's what my client told me after we both returned from separate vacations in Italy. This mutual experience allowed us to be on the same page; every room became its own little building within this town of sorts. We created a center hallway that operates as the main street, and every room has a unique view, ceiling, finishes; they almost feel like separate houses. Contributing to this feel is the fact that there are five levels to the house, but at no point within the home are there more than five or six stairs to climb; it all flows together rather seamlessly. It's such a fun and intriguing house that continues to develop from the owner's many travels.
Photograph by Patrick Banks, Candelaria Design

FACING PAGE TOP: The simple Spanish Colonial house will stand the test of time. It's the first home to be built in Silverleaf and is used to market and draw other residents to the area.
Photograph by Christiaan Blok

FACING PAGE BOTTOM: My clients wanted a ranch hacienda home, so we designed it as a series of rectangles. All the spaces are two-sided and flow to the outside and to an inner courtyard. What's fun is that the home is in the desert, but these inner courtyards create a lush and sequestered ambience. A fire pit overlooks the desert and operates well with the rustic swimming pool. Overall, the home blends in with the harsh desert landscape but also offers an intimate area of elegant retreat.
Photograph by Christiaan Blok

A native of Chicago, Erik Peterson, AIA, was inspired by the great homes and buildings of Frank Lloyd Wright and Louis Sullivan seen throughout the city, which duly influenced him to enter the architectural field. Erik earned his bachelor's in architecture from Iowa State University, pursued classical studies in Rome, interned in London and later received his master's from Arizona State. His love for Arizona took hold, and today Erik's firm, Peterson Architecture & Associates, founded in 2002, designs classic and contemporary residences and hospitality projects throughout the Southwest.

The firm's architectural approach is simple: it practices "regionalism." Erik and his cadre of accredited architects design to specific place using indigenous materials and styles appropriate to and inspired by the region. The firm's portfolio includes privately commissioned residences that exhibit beautiful form and function, designed to weather the extreme climate and integrate visually into the cactus-dotted desertscape. Each custom home has an exclusive resort feeling, undeniably informed by PAA's commercial experience designing premier luxury properties for J.W. Marriott, The Ritz-Carlton and others. In turn, the firm's fine hotel and resort spaces take on the comfortable feeling of home away from home, designs informed by PAA's custom residential work.

"We believe in the architectural approach of 'regionalism,' specific to place and an extension of the land."

—Erik Peterson

PETERSON ARCHITECTURE & ASSOCIATES

"Inspired by site, we design organic sustainable architecture using indigenous materials and regional styles for a home unique to its owners."

—Erik Peterson

RIGHT: The classical master bathroom exudes a luxury resort feeling. We designed it true to historical precedent but with a more formal Spanish Colonial influence. The second-story room has groin-vaulted ceilings, solid Italian marble columns and a hand-laid mosaic tile floor "rug." To bring the outdoors into the bedroom, a private patio deck design maximizes stunning views of desert mountains and sparkling city lights.
Photograph by Dino Tonn Photography

PREVIOUS PAGES: Following the principles of Wright, we limit materials to three; in this case we specified glass walls, copper overhangs and natural stone elements for the contemporary home's façade. We apply the same rule of three to dividing massing and grouping windows. Having worked with the Frank Lloyd Wright School of Architecture mentoring program and on projects while with Taliesin Architects, we believe in abiding by tried and true constructive principles. The home's indoor-outdoor patio experience features a symmetrical swimming pool hardscape. Regionalism personified, the design incorporates dry-stack rose quartzite walls without mortar for an organic effect.
Photographs by Pam Singleton

"Residential designs should be livable and highly personalized spaces, not generic box-like structures."

—Erik Peterson

ABOVE & FACING PAGE: We designed a traditional French Country-inspired home with a formal exterior façade and rustic elements to create an authentic farmhouse feeling in Phoenix. We collaborated with the interior designer and landscape architect to achieve flow and unity from inside to the outdoors. The sunny conservatory is enclosed by leaded beveled glass walls that serve as a beautiful visual screen; imported limestone floor tiles have charming ladybug and cricket insets for a rural garden touch. A dramatic entry foyer with its wide winding staircase leads to the home office. The formal family room with curved beam trusses adds Old World charm and is adjacent to the spacious kitchen. Our homes are extremely functional. We customize intimate spaces in the context of large-scale residences to realistically accommodate the needs of family life.

Photographs by Robert Reck

"We respect Frank Lloyd Wright's design principles as they apply to massing and materiality of design, whether the home is classical or contemporary."

—Erik Peterson

ABOVE & FACING PAGE: We designed a rural Mediterranean-inspired residence overlooking the fairway of a prestigious country club golf course. After careful site analysis, we nestled the home down slightly for great views of the course yet with complete poolside privacy. We laid out the home on a curved radius to ensure that the interior spaces would fully utilize the views. To form the historically correct interpretation, we artfully combined traditional materials, including a genuine stucco exterior, mud-set native stone derived from the site and imported clay tile roofing. Proven Frank Lloyd Wright design principles are applied to massing and materials, yet the design is quite classical. Striving to be sensitive to the environment, we designed the home in accordance with the city's green build guidelines by specifying sustainable products and systems.
Photographs by Dino Tonn Photography

"Thoughtful designs integrate homes into the natural desertscape, always with sustainability top of mind."

—Erik Peterson

ABOVE & FACING PAGE: To preserve the site's dramatic 500-year-old saguaro cactus, we integrated the home seamlessly around the venerable succulent. The whole house is curved and designed on a radius. We specified indigenous materials, including locally mined copper and site-quarried stone. Glass panels optimize hypnotic mountain-desert views. The south-facing front door enjoys copper overhangs to protect residents from the relentless sun's rays and reflect intense heat for added efficiency.

Photographs by Pam Singleton

Founded by designers Quinn Boesenecker and Ping To, Pinnacle Architectural Studio focuses on high-end custom homes. From the beginning, Quinn knew that he wanted to create a firm that would stand above the rest. Not subscribing to one style in particular, Pinnacle prides itself on being able to work with many styles ranging from modern to Mediterranean and traditional to contemporary.

Since 2000, the firm has designed homes for some of Las Vegas' most prestigious communities such as Anthem Country Club, Lake Las Vegas, MacDonald Highlands, Queensridge, Seven Hills, Southern Highlands and The Ridges. Each custom home design is a direct reflection of its residents' personal taste, desires and needs coupled with the neighborhood's design criteria.

From its inception the firm has focused on giving individual attention to each project. Quinn and Ping personally handle the design work, no matter how many projects are on the docket. Their hands-on approach results in one-of-a-kind custom homes that seamlessly incorporate the geography of Las Vegas with innovative architectural design.

"Incorporating a variety of elements and materials into the design creates depth and interest."

—Quinn Boesenecker

PINNACLE ARCHITECTURAL STUDIO

"Just as different homeowners require different designs, so do different neighborhoods. The best architects are flexible and allow all types of architecture to influence their work."

—Quinn Boesenecker

LEFT: The modern home of photographer Peter Lik features a kitchen with a 20-foot bamboo ceiling. A curved portion of the ceiling is completely suspended over the nucleus of the space to provide more definition, while a stone fireplace adds warmth and texture.
Photograph by Peter Lik

PREVIOUS PAGES: A Las Vegas home featuring an abundance of windows and an expansive wooden ceiling is angled to take advantage of breathtaking city views. A custom steel fireplace, accompanied by a custom steel hearth and mantel, serves as a major focal point for the great room but also acts as a major support for the rear of the home. The backyard features an infinity pool that overlooks a golf course, and beyond the course are magnificent views of The Red Rock Mountains and the ever sought-after Las Vegas strip.
Photographs by George Guttenburg

ABOVE: From the stainless steel backsplash to the xenon white light coves to the black granite countertops, Ted and Arlene Schlazer's custom home is a direct reflection of their personality and lifestyle—hip, yet classy, with an unmistakable modern edge.
Photograph by George Guttenburg

FACING PAGE TOP: We designed the beautiful Tuscan-style home in a "U" shape to protect it from the strong Las Vegas winds. The patio wraps inside the entire courtyard, and beyond the columns are large break-away doors that are able to open up and take advantage of better weather. Of course, the view of the Las Vegas strip cannot be forgotten and is only a step away. Just to the right sits a stairway that takes you up to a private patio with full views of the strip.
Photograph by George Guttenburg

FACING PAGE BOTTOM: The home was designed by our firm and built by Quinn as his personal home. A 24-foot glass wall completely disappears into a pocket to create a larger open space for entertaining that is both inside and outside. Limestone floors, bamboo ceilings and metal overhangs are just some of the elements that make the home truly unique.
Photograph by Sam Som

> "Each home should be an expression of the homeowner's personality and tastes. Therefore, no two homes are ever the same."
>
> —Quinn Boesenecker

TOP: A solid mahogany door is the focus of a grand front entry. Accented with solid stone columns, corbels and trim work, the entrance makes an elegant statement.
Photograph by Sam Som

MIDDLE: The home is known as the "house with legs" because of the columns that stretch out like a spider. These "legs" are not only aesthetic but provide structural support for the patio and the house itself. The result is a modern home that offers a sense of warmth.
Photograph by Eric Jamison

BOTTOM: An inviting private courtyard greets guests as they make their way to the front door. The courtyard also offers privacy to the rooms that look out onto it and creates serene views dictated by the design concept.
Photograph by George Guttenburg

FACING PAGE: A Mediterranean home features a classic combination of arched windows with surrounds, corbels and precast columns. We designed the home to be elongated and in turn married it with a 75-foot-wide pool with a disappearing edge angled toward the Las Vegas strip in order to provide breathtaking views.
Photograph by Eric Jamison

"The landscape of Las Vegas affords so many opportunities to take an innovative design approach. Every project offers new challenges and ways to express new ideas."

—Quinn Boesenecker

ABOVE: A copper frame accented with stonework marks the entrance of a Las Vegas home. The home's living room serves as a cozy receiving area and is accented by a two-story wood and metal fireplace as well as views of the spectacular Las Vegas strip.

FACING PAGE TOP: Copper, metal, stone and stucco work together to create a textured exterior while a custom iron and copper gate serves as the entrance into a luxurious courtyard.

FACING PAGE BOTTOM: A living room's trey ceiling is accented with metal, stacked stone, solid pieces of granite and wallpaper to create a warm and tactile atmosphere.
Photographs by George Guttenburg

Growing up in the small town of Emory with a population of a few hundred residents, David Shiflet inherited strong family roots with homegrown values. He reminisces about building outdoor playhouses with his grandmother, a farmwoman and creative carpenter who nurtured his imagination. But it was academic training while attending the University of Texas during the 1970s that had quite an influence on his career. Graduating from UT's renowned architectural program, David had earned the credentials and gained inspiration to become one of Austin's most respected architects.

He admires the work of legendary regional Texas architect O'Neil Ford and Charles Moore, who designed The Sea Ranch in California. Yet David has an appreciation for giants like Italian Renaissance architect Andrea Palladio and American visionary Frank Lloyd Wright. David and his professional team design in a variety of genres appropriate to clients' needs and desires. They love drawing both contemporary and traditional designs, masterfully creating structural and aesthetic perfection. David's passion embraces diverse styles, but were he to name a favorite vernacular, it would be cottage-style homes. Commissions have ranged from a cozy 900-square-foot lakeside retreat to a 30,000-square-foot castle. Examples of David's creative residential work dot Austin's landscape, many overlooking the Colorado River and on the hills above scenic Lake Travis.

"When a place of refuge is thoughtfully designed and crafted, it has power to stir emotions with its beauty."

—David Shiflet

SHIFLET GROUP ARCHITECTS, INC.

"The residents' vision is the most important thing to capture in architecture."

—David Shiflet

ABOVE & PREVIOUS PAGES: Inspired by Palladio's Villa Capra La Rotunda in northern Italy, our residential design was meant for a family with a formal lifestyle. The impressive home can be viewed from all four sides. Its classical lines and grand symmetry, cut limestone façade and authentic details handmade by artisans create a luxurious feeling, yet the home possesses a contemporary attitude. The Italian-American client had a definite vision, and we worked for three years to complete the palazzo. Situated on a 16-acre estate overlooking Lake Travis, the peninsula home is an architectural jewel.

FACING PAGE: The residence is set on a hilltop and has two expansive back terraces to allow for wonderful outdoor dining replete with picturesque vistas. We designed the living room's 30-foot-high Venetian plaster domed ceiling on axis with the domed Texas state capitol downtown, which is clearly visible through a trio of arched windows from the front door.
Photographs by Casey Dunn

"Cottage homes should have a handmade quality, slightly imperfect yet well-crafted."

—David Shiflet

RIGHT: We designed an intimate cottage, a one-story wonder with handmade quality and charm that suits its lakeside location. An adjacent guesthouse and separate office structure with seven-car garage creates a small-scale compound perfect for weekend relaxation. We achieved its storybook look with a natural fieldstone chimney and hearth, flagstone walkway and front porch. Quirky uneven wood siding and wooden sashed windows give the home a regional Texas flavor that blends beautifully in context with its Lake Travis setting.
Photograph by Casey Dunn

> "A well-designed home should fit today's lifestyle but endure for generations."
>
> —David Shiflet

TOP: Informal yet traditional, the Tuscan-style country kitchen reflects the home's authentic exterior design. In keeping with the Italianate style, imported Carerra marble countertops and handmade floor tiles were incorporated. We planned the custom-crafted hardwood cabinetry and antiqued cook's island—functional elements with a refined aesthetic perfect for the sophisticated homeowner-chef.
Photograph by Casey Dunn

BOTTOM: An open kitchen plan with medieval wooden beamed ceilings and tiny windows creates a castle-like atmosphere in the Old World-inspired residence. Natural materials and handcrafted European influences are evident in the architecture we create, but current lifestyle needs are always met with practical configurations of space.
Photograph by Tre Dunham

FACING PAGE: The welcoming courtyard with its charming, gated stone archway leads to the French Country manor. We designed the private estate for a young, active family with children and pets, so the home is upscale but eclectic and relaxed in true Southern style. Native Austin limestone and a genuine slate roof define the home. A detached office, multicar garage and adjacent guest and pool houses were designed to create a rural village effect.
Photograph by Mark Knight

"When classical architectural principles are followed and genuine materials are used, truth is revealed."

—David Shiflet

ABOVE: Like an ancient Moorish castle with turrets and towers, mottled stone walls and copper roofing, the custom design captures the aesthetic of its inhabitants. Gothic windows and solid wooden doors exhibit authenticity and beauty based on historical precedent.
Photograph by Tre Dunham

FACING PAGE: We rely on artisans with world-class skills to execute residential designs in fine detail. Talented wrought-iron craftsmen, millworkers and stonecutters transform our blueprints into works of art. Stenciled antique pine timbers, handcarved mantels, bespoke ironwork and vaulted ceilings are marks of a well-designed home. We specified automated glass walls for a ranch home's indoor-outdoor great room featuring Boveda ceilings and engineered an impressive 4,000-pound, tapered stone room for a French estate.
Top left, top right & bottom left photographs by Casey Dunn
Bottom right photograph by Mark Knight

Preston Wood is known for his extraordinary design solutions. His range of expertise includes designing affordable small houses, stately mansions, master planned urban dwellings and townhomes in the heart of Houston, throughout the suburbs and across the United States. The accomplished residential designer majored in architecture and construction management and immediately began developing a thriving residential design business; this experience gave him the ability to not only conceptualize great architectural plans but to create them with utmost imagination for more than 30 years.

The well-versed designer does not repeat one style or regional vernacular. He embraces each client's vision and works in all genres, bringing dreams to fruition. Research is gathered from trips to European cities and studies of early New England architecture. Whether designing a Victorian townhome on a small lot or a sprawling Italian-inspired mansion on wooded acreage, Preston is sure to take full advantage of nature's topography. Inspiration springs from both positive and negative aspects of a site; home designs are seamlessly integrated into their natural surroundings. Advocates of green building with a broad understanding of construction complexities, the Preston Wood & Associates team is ready to meet the most demanding building challenges while defining luxury lifestyles.

"High density dwellings in urban settings should be designed to maximize great views as well as provide a sense of privacy for homeowners."

—Preston Wood

PRESTON WOOD & ASSOCIATES

"Design inspiration springs from the land; every site has something to minimize or take advantage of."

—Preston Wood

ABOVE: Great arched windows, box-beamed ceilings and a two-way limestone fireplace come together to create the perfect living room experience.
Photograph by T.K. Images

FACING PAGE: We strive to take advantage of the site, capturing its best features. For example, a spectacular garden or pool view is captured through windows that reflect arched details of the exterior façade. Open and flooded with light, the environment offers a grand feeling of spaciousness. A library-study enjoys volume and light yet the space has an ambience of intimacy with separate work areas and a comfortable reading cove.
Photographs by Stephen Gutierrez

PREVIOUS PAGES: Our eight-acre master planned community was inspired by a village in Andalusia, Spain. The townhomes have a minimal footprint with their four-story vertical design. This small footprint provided the additional green space to create a large central park, complete with fountain, as well as radiating finger parks offering a majority of the 118 homes views of the lush grounds. Roof terraces allow for magnificent skyline views, yet tower structures provide a sense of privacy. An authentic Spanish influence is evident in the simple, well-proportioned design of this townhome community with its continental flair.
Photograph by Rob Muir

"An irregular piece of land may call for a very specific footprint that demands artful planning and efficient design; such complexities are invigorating."

—Preston Wood

ABOVE: We established a traditional look and feel for a residence built on an asymmetrical site. A wide-angle view from the dining room through the living room captures the curved staircase and many interior architectural elements. We work to create an open, dramatic area within narrow configurations but with well-defined living spaces.
Photograph by T.K. Images

FACING PAGE: An authentic New Orleans-style garden home features wide porches that allow residents and guests to fully enjoy views of the downtown skyline. The visual expanse across the living room showcases the relationship of five varying levels; from the living room you can see the entry foyer as well as the overlooking breakfast room. Architecturally open living spaces make the narrow three-story home's rooms appear extraordinarily large yet comfortable and intimate.
Photographs by Rob Muir

Gearheart Construction Co., page 79   S&R Development, page 89

the structure

chapter two

Desert Star Construction, page 67

Gearheart Construction Co., page 79

Desert Star Construction, page 67

It is passion that fuels Jerry Meek, who has been instilled with a strong work ethic and an entrepreneurial spirit since childhood. He started his own tree-trimming business at age 14, founded his carpentry business at 19, and then became a general contractor in 1985. Today, Desert Star Construction is a family-owned business that provides clientele with unparalleled building services in an atmosphere of integrity.

The firm's outstanding reputation has been earned; Jerry's company is renowned for its impeccable, custom work performed throughout Paradise Valley and the north Scottsdale communities. Utilizing skilled craftsmen and suppliers from Arizona and around the world, Jerry collaborates with respected architects, interior designers, lighting designers and landscape architects throughout the region. The company delivers premier-quality residential construction services, and its true hallmark is an ability to create a diversity of styles. Commissions range from unique, private dwellings to luxurious Personal Resorts℠ exceeding 40,000 square feet. Desert Star team members pride themselves on using state-of-the-art systems, innovative technologies and beautiful, authentic materials. But it is Jerry's expert eye for flawless detail and uncompromising craftsmanship that has kept his firm brightly shining for more than three decades.

"The design goal must be a true reflection of the owners; crafting unique, innovative homes, while building relationships with passion and integrity defines the creative process."

—Jerry Meek

DESERT STAR CONSTRUCTION

"We believe in building green so homeowners can live green."

—Jerry Meek

RIGHT & PREVIOUS PAGES: We created an Italian villa ambience through Old World architecture and authentic materials, both in the interior rooms and exterior façade. We used reclaimed wood beams, recycled interior and exterior doors, imported flooring and ancient roof tiles for the home and sourced many stone artifacts for fountains and water features. The exterior is augmented with Italian plaster and limestone in keeping with the Tuscan aesthetic. We constructed the energy-efficient home using eco-alternative Rastra, a sustainable, recycled material that offers superior insulation and a high fire rating; the walls are of varied thicknesses ideal for architectural massing. Our homes are meant to last for generations, and we use green elements whenever possible. Architecture by Oz Architects. Interior design by Karen Rapp Interiors.

Photographs by Mark Boisclair

ABOVE: We renovated a contemporary home set on a hillside with limited accessibility. A complex, cantilevered roof structure was erected to allow for automated sliding doors; homeowners now enjoy a 270-degree mountain view from the master bedroom. We added a spa and fire pit surrounded by natural stone with an invisible-edge swimming pool for a refreshing oasis. Cutting-edge technology is used in every home so homeowners find it easy to manage. Architecture by Christy Wareing. Interior design by David Michael Miller.
Photograph by Bill Timmerman

ABOVE TOP & BOTTOM: The recreational basement features a colorful children's playroom with guest bleachers and built-in storage. We worked with the interior designer who incorporated a wall mural, checkerboard tile, pinwheel rugs and fabric sail ceilings. The old-time streetscape was built onsite by our craftsmen to create a colorful storefront for each child. We also constructed an adjacent movie theater complete with lobby and ticket booth, a game room and fitness center for more family fun. Architecture by The Coffman Group. Interior design by Elizabeth Rosensteel Design.
Photographs by Robert Reck

"The bookends of success are starting with a plan and finishing to perfection."

—Jerry Meek

ABOVE LEFT & RIGHT: We assembled the imported, oversized stone mantel in the living room, and the artisan-made wrought iron handrail was also created onsite. Venetian plaster walls and hand-scraped hardwood floors are a seamless backdrop for our custom focal points. We installed a hand-carved stone hood and surround with backsplash for Old World charm while hand-scraped walnut floors complement the ceiling's hewn wood beams. Architecture by Dick Reece. Interior design by Bruce Stadola.
Photographs by Mark Boisclair

FACING PAGE TOP: Our team built a high-tech fitness room with a European feel. We placed operable steel-sash, putty-glazed casement windows in the center of the space for proper ventilation. The window walls provide breathtaking mountain views. Architecture by Oz Architects. Interior design by Vallone Design and Karen Rapp Interiors.
Photograph by Mark Boisclair

FACING PAGE BOTTOM: A newly constructed traditional kitchen features reclaimed beams, wide-plank English oak floors, steel windows and a poured zinc countertop for refined beauty and longevity. Architecture by Peterson Architecture. Interior design by Vallone Design.
Photograph by Dino Tonn Photography

PREVIOUS PAGES: Our dream team can build the extraordinary. Beyond custom homes, we specialize in Personal Resorts℠ with all of the amenities one would find in a five-star property away from home. Ideal for formal entertaining, the rural Mediterranean-inspired estate includes the spacious main residence, a 16-car garage for the homeowner-collector, a detached guesthouse and a tennis and pool pavilion with convenient outdoor shower. Artfully landscaped grounds sport a putting green, tee boxes, regulation tennis court, classic lap pool and spa amid manicured lawns and stone walkways for the ultimate desert escape. Architecture by Candelaria Design. Landscape architecture by Berghoff Design Group. Interior design by Bruce Stadola.
Photograph by AZ Chopper Cam

"Using authentic materials creates an ambience true to the home's architectural aesthetic."

—Jerry Meek

LEFT: Inspired by a Mediterranean materials palette, our craftsmen constructed the façade using reclaimed stone window and door surrounds, wood beams and clay roof tiles from France; even antique stairs have new castings of period railings for authenticity. All of the steel windows were putty-glazed onsite to bring a genuine European look. We are passionate about meticulous attention to detail. Our quality assurance means building it right the first time. Architecture by Oz Architects. Interior design by Vallone Design and Karen Rapp Interiors.
Photograph by Mark Boisclair

Relationship-building is Joe Gearheart's forte. He has mastered the art of working closely with homeowners, architects and the design community to create some of Fort Worth's most illustrious residences. What comes naturally to Joe has become an integral part of the firm's philosophy: a commitment to teamwork. His professional approach underscores the importance of mutual respect for loyal employees, designers, vendors and subcontractors working as a cohesive team on each project.

The firm prides itself on presenting realistic estimates and timelines for each private home commission. A presence in the custom home industry for more than 40 years, the Gearheart firm has built a reputation on quality and integrity, from new homes to renovations, additions to remodels. Exclusive homebuilding and extended home maintenance is a dual specialty; the Gearheart name is synonymous with home maintenance, and the firm offers to look after each dwelling throughout its lifespan.

Attention to detail may stem from Joe's formal education—undergraduate work in both engineering and economics coupled with an MBA—but his dedication to achieving a refined aesthetic for homeowners is his passion. Perfectionist execution and value-engineering are both strong suits; the firm's cadre of 35 proven professionals and partnerships with top architects, designers and artisans have made the Gearheart name one that connotes impeccable standards in the luxury homebuilding genre.

"The best residential designs are executed according to the architectural plans in close relationship with homeowners and all associated professionals."

—Joe Gearheart

GEARHEART CONSTRUCTION CO.

TOP: A teardown project, the new home was built on an existing foundation so we were able to save the mature landscaping and use the same footprint. The fireplace was not demolished, saving time and money, while white oak plank flooring and paneling were handcrafted by Mario Camilleri.
Photograph by Danny Piassick

BOTTOM: We redefined the back entrance with a harmonic convergence of limestone, brick and 16-inch-wide, stained fir beams, creating an archway carved out of wood, assembled and joined. The terrace is accented with solid, ornamental wrought-iron guard railings. Interior designer Leigh Taylor and architecture firm Collison Design Group were instrumental in the home's success.
Photograph by Danny Piassick

FACING PAGE TOP: Dramatically remodeled, the home includes arched ceilings with schoolhouse lights, glass shelving inspired by a Parisian bakery and a gourmet chef-quality 600-pound stainless steel island. The green-painted millwork and paneling are by Mario Camilleri.
Photograph by Danny Piassick

FACING PAGE BOTTOM: The elegant transitional-style dining room features custom Marvin clad-wood windows and doors, whitewashed oak flooring and an exquisite chandelier with additional wall sconce lighting effects. The home has 25 pastel and bolder hues on millwork, sheetrock and wood trim. Julie Hayes, the interior designer-owner, calls her home her "color lab." Architecture by Joe Self, AIA.
Photograph by Danny Piassick

PREVIOUS PAGES LEFT: Designed in a contemporary Texas Hill Country vernacular, the multilevel stucco, metalwork and glass structure was an engineering feat as it sits on a site that slopes upward and required serious retaining walls. In collaboration with architects at Smith, Ekblad & Associates and interior designer Sherry Hayslip, we built the home from the ground up and ensured that its timeless aesthetic carried through to every detail.
Photograph by Ira Montgomery

PREVIOUS PAGES RIGHT: The Santa Fe-inspired contemporary residence—designed by Roger Dobbins, AIA, of Dobbins-Crow Architects—features distressed natural fir beams that we precisely aligned with the fireplace. We covered the walls in soft, ivory-colored American Clay material for a fine-textured, nontoxic and sustainable treatment. The interior design is by Jean Smith Design.
Photograph by Danny Piassick

"Renovations in historic neighborhoods should be seamlessly integrated so that the new structures look as if they've always been there."

—Joe Gearheart

LEFT: The charming 1936 Spanish hacienda is situated on seven acres in a premier Fort Worth neighborhood; we restored several rooms to integrate flawlessly with the existing architecture.

FACING PAGE TOP: The architect put a contemporary spin on a traditional historic kitchen. The floor is antique Mexican tile but the custom wood cabinetry and the butcher-block island are finished with high-gloss auto body paint. Sophisticated countertops made of dark gray distressed soapstone add contrast.

FACING PAGE BOTTOM: Through the 70-year history of the hacienda, some of the renovations and technical upgrades had not been done in the most artistic manner. Our team had to re-run gas and electric service entrances to return the home to its original design. The entrance courtyard and exposed rafter-tail eave of the home now looks as it did 70 years ago. We built wooden rafters and the loggia to create a shady haven so as not to affect the vintage clay tile roof. Irregular shapes of Lueders limestone were honed to form the patio floor while stacked stone steps remain natural. The architecture and interior design are by Blake Goble, AIA, of the New York-based firm B Space.
Photographs by Danny Piassick

"Through focused collaboration with architects, designers and craftspeople, the desired aesthetic is achieved successfully."

—Joe Gearheart

ABOVE: To integrate the residence thoughtfully into its site, the architect started from the bottom and worked up. Natural stone covers the base of the home and straight grain fir is pressure-treated to weather the intense Texas sun and lakeside moisture. The steeply terraced yard was created from indigenous Palo Pinto sandstone in interesting shades of brown, caramel and tan.

FACING PAGE: Perched on a cliff over Eagle Mountain Lake, the contemporary home showcases seven species of wood contrasted by white sheetrock material. It has circular forms and lots of glass, but most of the home is rectilinear in layout. The architecture and interior design are by Mark Gunderson, AIA; Mario Camilleri did the artisan millwork.
Photographs by Danny Piassick

"Our objective mirrors the architect's vision as we work in harmony to build a masterpiece and bring the homeowner's dream into reality."

—Joe Gearheart

LEFT: In the grand entrance of this luxurious home, the elliptical shaped crown and ceiling trim is plaster. This residence has 16 carved limestone columns with precast Corinthian capitals. Foyer details include Lueders limestone tiles with black granite diamonds. Hand-forged ironwork railings were commissioned to decorate the unique elliptical arc of the mansion stairway.

FACING PAGE TOP: The classic French estate's symmetrical exterior elevation features carved Lueders limestone and stucco over concrete block construction. Lead-coated copper dormers, gutters and downspouts have a deep gray matte finish for a refined European look. We employed Old World techniques throughout, from the slate roof to the carved stone frieze and balustrades.

FACING PAGE BOTTOM: Replete with millwork by Martin Grunow, the traditional French kitchen boasts mahogany cabinetry, a paneled refrigerator and a work island with European-quality craftsmanship. Polished marble countertops and a generous island are perfect for food preparation and large-scale entertaining. We collaborated on the project with Roger Dobbins, AIA, of Dobbins-Crow Architects and the interior design firm Elizabeth White Design.
Photographs by Danny Piassick

All of S&R Development's exclusive projects benefit from principal Saad Chehabi's decades of interior design, homebuilding and stonework experience, not to mention his perfectionist spirit and passion for architecture. Saad takes a unique approach, focusing on the architectural details and intricacies of each home. Traveling to Europe several times a year, namely France and Italy, he collects authentic antique pieces such as decorative ironwork, hand-carved stone mantels and friezes and beautiful wood elements that can be artfully incorporated into new constructions.

Collaborating closely with architects, Saad provides valuable input to conceptualize floorplans and refine façades with elegant details. His signature designs emphasize an inviting traffic flow with oversized windows for natural light. A multifaceted builder, Saad also advises clientele in selecting furnishings and can readily design an original stone mosaic wall or elaborate inlaid floor while also lending his expertise in lighting and landscape design. His company builds French châteaux and Tuscan-inspired villas with authentic natural materials and exquisite finishes; the result is museum-quality perfection. Saad's philosophy goes beyond fine craftsmanship—he treasures every project as his own, ensuring that the design-build process is as enjoyable as the final masterpiece.

"Authenticity is established through using the finest materials imported from Europe and by emulating highly detailed Old World craftsmanship."

—Saad Chehabi

S&R DEVELOPMENT

"Antique French limestone, marble from Italy and Spain and unique hand-carved mantels are elements that distinguish a home."

—Saad Chehabi

LEFT & PREVIOUS PAGES: Authentic, hand-carved stone has an aesthetic that far surpasses cast-stone details. To design residences reminiscent of palaces, museums and homes of nobility, we source exquisite architectural details like solid onyx columns, antique Italian stone fireplaces, inlaid onyx and limestone flooring—one-of-a-kind elements that make a formal living room come to life. We specify wall finishes such as genuine Venetian plaster to accentuate groin-vaulted ceilings and Italianesque lighting fixtures.
Photographs courtesy of S&R Development

"Inspiration stems from nature's organic shapes or multicultural designs of antiquity."

—Saad Chehabi

LEFT & FACING PAGE: Seasoned stonework experts present homeowners with elegant design options inspired by ancient mosaics. Blending the natural coloration of variegated marble pieces with smooth limestone, we design and creatively construct beautiful patterns and ornate motifs to enhance the interior space. *Photographs courtesy of S&R Development*

"The exterior façade must exhibit authentic details, expressing the architectural genre in its purest form."

—Saad Chehabi

ABOVE & FACING PAGE: We delineated the rear elevation of a timeless Mediterranean home with a wraparound balcony featuring imported solid limestone columns, custom decorative ironwork and an antique-finish clay tile roof. Uncompromising quality and meticulously detailed workmanship ensure that the home will endure for generations.
Photographs courtesy of S&R Development

"A home's character is defined through its architectural details."

—Saad Chehabi

RIGHT & FACING PAGE: Refined architectural details dignify interior and exterior spaces. Whether we design and build library bookcases of reclaimed wood and hand-paint them to resemble those seen in a grand Venetian home or construct a courtyard hardscape replete with sculptural swimming pool, the beauty of authenticity and fine craftsmanship is apparent. It may take weeks for artisans to create a custom inlaid floor of black marble and cream limestone mosaic, but the exceptional museum-quality effect is well worth the time.
Photographs courtesy of S&R Development

"Transforming spaces into timeless, lifestyle-friendly places is the ultimate interior design goal."

—Jane-Page Crump

elements of structure

chapter three

Founded in 1977 Jane Page Design Group is one of Houston's most illustrious and industry-respected design firms, creating interior transformations in prominent private residences throughout the region. Jane-Page Crump, ASID, is the studio's founder, president and lead designer. The award-winning, full-service interior design firm is well known for its elegant and distinctive work. For more than three decades, the creativity and uncompromising standards of Jane Page Design Group have made the firm one of the most sought-after by informed clientele. The firm's exquisite interiors speak to Jane-Page's exceptional talent, knowledge and experience, demonstrating utmost creative savvy whether designing traditional, richly appointed rooms or interpreting more contemporary expressions.

The professional design firm is committed to serving high-profile patrons; its roster includes many Fortune 500 executives, celebrities and political notables. Jane-Page's established company has always fostered a collaborative approach—the design team partners closely with clientele, working in tandem with the finest contractors and tenured architects to ensure that dream interiors are realized. Above all, Jane-Page strives to interpret each client's vision by translating needs and desires into impeccable living spaces that exemplify beautiful form and function.

JANE PAGE DESIGN GROUP

ABOVE: We transformed an ordinary space into a formal, classical master bath. It features gorgeous cabinets and millwork that are painted and glazed to add depth to a neutral palette. We used a unique combination of stone tile with standard and basketweave mosaics. Hand-cut, contrasting stone borders add texture; a similar motif is repeated on the custom-etched and beveled mirror panels above the vanity and in the leaded glass window. Details matter—plush towels are monogrammed to reflect the same decorative style.

FACING PAGE: Our challenge was to create a peaceful retreat for residents in the master bedroom. We designed a custom coffee bar and refrigerator hidden within cabinetry as well as a display niche for family photos and collections. A tailored chaise lounge with swivel club chairs presents a fireside vignette for reading and relaxing. For ultimate privacy, a motorized blackout shade is discreetly housed in the crown valance. The bedding's damask pattern was repeated in the shaped valance to frame the window view while mirroring the vibrant hues of the lush garden.

PREVIOUS PAGES: We designed the living room as a true family-friendly space that exudes casual sophistication. A grand-scale, carved stone fireplace is the focal point between custom alder wood cabinets. We concealed the plasma television behind pocket doors with extra storage below for electronics and gaming accessories. Muted tones and soft textures unify the space; a curved sectional, framed lounge chairs and swivel chairs provide comfortable seating. Our custom-fabricated area rug anchors the room with its graceful leaf pattern, which is forgiving to minor spills.

Photographs by Bruce Bennett

"Proper materials, handcrafted elements and superior selections all work together to create a sense of luxury."

—Jane-Page Crump

RIGHT: We faced the entire range wall with natural stone since a heat-resistant wall had not been addressed in the blueprints. Our design team worked with the homebuilder to resolve the issue by designing the authentic, dramatic surround. The light, gray-toned stone reflects the home's château-style exterior façade while providing a backdrop for the handcrafted, French limestone hood. Custom elements abound along with the latest high-end appliances, including a professional Wolf range and built-in Sub-Zero refrigerator.

Photograph by Bruce Bennett

"Exquisite rooms emerge when architecture, textiles, original art and high technology are integrated."

—Jane-Page Crump

ABOVE: Hand-carved dragons flank the theater's screen; we commissioned Indonesian artists to craft every detail. The room's large dentil crown was inspired by a castle fortress. Our local artisans applied layered faux finishes on walls to achieve the effect of aged stone. The room's low ceiling features fiber-optic stars framed by false beams to give an illusion of height. We designed creative lighting using a combination of low-voltage, incandescent, ambient and fiber optic elements. Custom torchiere sconces and low-voltage fixtures accent the walls and valance while vertical halogen clips and recessed low-voltage spots dramatically highlight the dragon sculptures. Curtains, lights and audiovisual equipment are remote-controlled on the Crestron touchpad system.

FACING PAGE: Our classic gentleman's den expresses the finer things in life: dark walnut paneling, rare books and hand-rolled cigars. The handsome room required a special ventilation system to promote air quality; we designed a unique built-in humidor behind raw Mexican cedar doors. Strategic lighting showcases the rich paneling and stunning, hand-finished Versailles floors. We used adjustable low-voltage fixtures to accent the walls and paintings; recessed lighting inside beams allows for reading and entertaining. A single touchpad allows all fixtures to be remote-controlled individually.
Photographs by Bruce Bennett

"Each project is a new adventure. Challenges inspire us to embark on the creative journey in search of perfection."

—Jane-Page Crump

ABOVE & FACING PAGE: We positioned an outdoor stone fountain as a window focal point to be clearly seen upon entering the master bath. The design team transformed the generous room into a warm, comfortable spa-like respite with stained wood trim, glazed finishes, patterned marble tile and subtle, textural wallcoverings. The glamorous oversized mirrors were precisely cut and beveled to fit with architectural pilasters; one panel cleverly conceals a flat-screen television. The vanity mirrors draw attention upward to the clerestory windows, emphasizing the room's overall sense of spaciousness. We cut the towering wall height by installing Reed and Ribbon decorative wood moulding.

Photographs by Rob Muir

"Creative lighting design is the finishing touch that defines an interior."

—Jane-Page Crump

ABOVE: We designed an urban kitchen of distinction with golden travertine floors and Wood-Mode custom cherry wood cabinets; authentic carved stone and brick pavers surround the range. A large-scale chef's preparation island and sink area provide excellent work space with polished granite surfaces, and custom beveled glass windows bring in needed natural light while adding interest and screening street traffic. We incorporated leaded, beveled glass in the upper cabinet niches to mimic the windows; the niches are illuminated with fiber optics. The impressive nine-foot-tall cabinetry wall displays kitchenware, houses wine, provides storage and boasts an appliance garage and concealed television. Our curvilinear cabinet solution creates a clutter-free zone that graciously invites traffic flow into the dining space.
Photograph by Hall Pucket

FACING PAGE: We reinvented the traditional paneled library using rare macassar ebony combined with cherry wood millwork; its bookcase doors have linear black accents for contrast. We specified gorgeous cherry wood floors with ornate borders of brass, marble and lacewood inlays. Our custom spiral staircase connects library levels with hand-forged iron balusters that reiterate the home's foyer railing design. Craftsmen covered the oval, domed ceiling in a layered metallic finish with stunning hand-stenciled designs. Artistic lighting effects further enhance the room's details. A centered, wrought-iron chandelier brings the domed ceiling to life. The cabinet crown houses low-voltage lighting to highlight pilasters, and vertical clip lights cast a soft glow throughout. Library lighting is easily controlled and dimmed on the sophisticated Lutron system.
Photographs by Rob Muir

"Authentic tiles handcrafted by skilled artisans give incomparable beauty to a home."

—Terri Boyd

ABOVE: Handmade encaustic tiles feature natural grey and ochre-colored clay; the pieces are inlaid to form a checkerboard pattern. We used encaustic tiles for unique beauty and texture because the pattern on the surface is not a product of the glaze but of different colors of clay. The dimensional trim and ropes finish off the wainscot effect with a refined appearance.
Photograph courtesy of Vallone Design

FACING PAGE: Our custom tile mural above the range is a true work of art. We commissioned an artisan who trained in Portugal and is well-versed in the traditional Majolica process with its Neapolitan style and spirit. The original hand-painted, hand-glazed backsplash with a vivid yellow bird and leafy tree design is the room's focal point.
Photograph courtesy of Bouton & Foley Interiors, Inc.

"Ancient tile-making methods have become lost arts; we search globally to offer a diverse selection."

—Terri Boyd

TOP: Inspired by a Medici frieze with classical Italian Renaissance imagery, we adapted the look to create an exotic custom tile design for the hood. An unusual pair of griffin figures adorns the backsplash centerpiece above the cooktop.
Photograph courtesy of Leila Armstrong, Winssinger Interior Design

MIDDLE & BOTTOM: We recommended interesting textural, encausted tiles to form the preparation island's durable, sealed surface. In keeping with the rustic theme, the range backsplash features tiles in an original harlequin diamond pattern. A custom hand-painted, hand-glazed tile mural showcases the homeowner's stylized barn with checkerboard borders.
Middle photograph courtesy of Avril Interiors
Bottom photograph courtesy of Bouton & Foley Interiors, Inc.

FACING PAGE: By combining material from three different tilemakers, we created a unique and exciting backsplash. The red and white checkerboard tile pattern was designed using a made-to-order line that offers a vast color palette for unlimited possibilities. The new vibrant red pigment in the glaze is safe for the environment. A hand-painted border accents the backsplash.
Photograph courtesy of Wiseman and Gale Interiors

"Colorful, textured, matte or highly glazed, handcrafted tile lends personality to a room."

—Terri Boyd

ABOVE LEFT & RIGHT: Tile work can be integrated as an accent or as the dominating centerpiece of a room. Our design features encaustic, handmade tiles framed with dimensional trim for an exotic Maltese influence. The Moroccan-inspired backsplash with six-inch square tiles created a large-scale, two-color pattern with the band on the hood in the same pattern but done in a relief tile to create texture.
Left photograph courtesy of Wiseman and Gale Interiors
Right photograph courtesy of K.J. Patterson, Tile Artisan

FACING PAGE: We brought the Spanish-style casita kitchen to life with an unexpected combination of vibrant colors: blue, gold, burgundy, green and orange. Bold-hued tiles enriched with complex, multi-layered glazes were installed to create an eye-catching effect; some tiles have impressions, and the glazing further delineates the design.
Photograph courtesy of Wiseman and Gale Interiors

"Hand-painted tile and mosaic stonework can express both classical and contemporary tastes."

—Terri Boyd

RIGHT: The powder room is a prime example of pressed and cured cement tile work still made in the Old World method as seen in Morocco or the South of France. Today this durable tile is made in the Dominican Republic and Mexico. The imported tiles have a high-contrast black and white pattern for a stunning artistic effect, but they can be made in any color combination or pattern.
Photograph courtesy of Terese Messina Interiors

FACING PAGE TOP: We created an ambience of antiquity using unglazed terracotta tile from Spain, which was stained with linseed oil and sealed. Bas relief tiles at the base of the tub give a sculptural effect, and miniature tiles are inlaid and edged with dimensional mouldings to add more interest to the walls. By varying tile sizes, shapes and layout, we transformed the custom spa and shower room into a castle-like retreat.
Photograph courtesy of Melinda Chipley, Designer

FACING PAGE BOTTOM LEFT & RIGHT: We designed the stone mosaic wraparound curve and tile backsplash as an elegant backdrop for a polished white Calcutta Gold marble bath. Embossed relief tiles add drama to a new installation; matte glazed and antique-finish arabesque shapes can be cut out like lace or filled in to change the look.
Left photograph courtesy of Bruce Stodolla Interiors
Right photograph courtesy of Wiseman and Gale Interiors

"Drawing an original design suited to the space is the first step to creating a tile and stone mosaic masterpiece."

—Terri Boyd

ABOVE LEFT & RIGHT: Soft-toned river rocks line the outdoor shower while coordinating stone mouldings define its architectural shape; we created a custom floor tile pattern to fit the small space. Cut and tumbled natural stones come in 12-inch squares that interlock for seamless flooring with charming country cottage ambience.

Left photograph courtesy of Bouton & Foley Interiors, Inc.
Right photograph courtesy of Wiseman and Gale Interiors

FACING PAGE: Custom handcrafted tiles make a unique style statement. We designed a decorative "skirt" to hide plumbing fixtures and covered it with stone mosaic to match the counters. An artfully inlaid backsplash with a fleur-de-lis repeat motif from edge to edge has major impact.
Photograph courtesy of Melinda Chipley, Designer

JULIAN'S FINE CABINETRY AND DESIGN

"High quality and sophistication never go out of style."

—Karen Doerflien

ABOVE & FACING PAGE: Because we work so closely with the homeowners, architects and designers, our cabinets blend seamlessly with the home. We use light-toned finishes to create bright, open kitchens yet maintain the warmth that people often want to create.

Photographs courtesy of Julian's Fine Cabinetry and Design

"Cabinetry has a wide range of possibilities—more than many homeowners realize. Nearly any color or finish can work if it's done properly."

—Mark Doerflien

LEFT & FACING PAGE: Whether we're designing for a traditional home with a large family or for a modern loft with a single resident, the spaces reflect both practical needs and artistic tastes. High quality and elegance come across in every space we design.
Photographs courtesy of Julian's Fine Cabinetry and Design

"We unite four elements: form, function, style and comfort."

—Mark Doerflien

ABOVE & FACING PAGE: Ornate, hand-carved cabinets and furniture-quality finishes create the richest environments. We work with more than 20 manufacturers and use local artisans to provide ultra customized work. Nothing is off limits. Homeowners love our variety—exotic woods, exclusive veneers and any number of specialty finishes.

Photographs courtesy of Julian's Fine Cabinetry and Design

RIGHT: For homeowners who wanted to bring sophistication to the bathroom, we created the perfect space. Initially they had a hard time visualizing what the finished product would look like, but our process let them see exactly what the outcome would be. Our CAD drawings include elevations plus top and side views, allowing every last detail to come through.

Photograph courtesy of Julian's Fine Cabinetry and Design

"People forget that cabinets aren't just for kitchens. Beautiful cabinetry works anywhere in a home."

—Karen Doerflien

RIGHT & FACING PAGE: Our designs create simple organization in rooms that can often become the most cluttered. Think of customized cabinetry in dressing areas, laundry rooms, libraries, wine cellars and mudrooms—it's the ideal solution to provide graceful storage spaces.

Photographs courtesy of Julian's Fine Cabinetry and Design

Phoenix, Arizona

"There is an art to tile and stonework design. Whether sleek or traditional, quiet Zen or exotic Moroccan, quality craftsmanship and originality make a lasting impression.

—Michele Kalec

ABOVE: We created the defining hardscape elements and paved the way to the outdoor living room with a luxurious poolside deck made of genuine reclaimed Chicago brick. Beyond the pool, a custom marble mosaic fountain wall has a subtle black chain pattern and arched radius back; natural limestone caps were custom-fabricated for both fountain and pool coping for a unifying effect.

FACING PAGE: The minimalist marble fireplace is the living room's centerpiece. Our artisans created the custom mantel and surround featuring an inlaid black granite pinstripe in contrast to the pure white Thassos marble slab fabrication. Simple and understated in design, the impression is sophisticated, contemporary, elegant.
Photographs by Adam Rodriguez, Adamsphoto

"Flawless craftsmanship can only be achieved with seasoned tile and stone artisans working in collaboration with respected architects, builders and designers."

—Michele Kalec

LEFT & FACING PAGE: We work diligently to create exceptional kitchens and baths, executing the interior design vision to perfection. Imported tiles and slab marble of superior quality were used for their intrinsic beauty and endurance. Large marble pieces were hand-cut to precision and artfully hand-laid by our master craftsmen to provide designs of distinction. Flooring, backsplashes, shower walls, vanities and countertops all enjoy the soft, refined chic that only natural marble and stone impart. Herzlinger Interiors provided these designs.
Photographs by Adam Rodriguez, Adamsphoto

"Intricate tile and stonework accents a home with beauty, grace and, above all, originality."

—Michele Kalec

ABOVE: Our pièce de résistance is a one-of-a-kind, boutique pool bar crafted from tile and mosaic. A massive slab of Jurassic green granite from Brazil was fabricated into the curvilinear bar top with an elegant edge profile. Ordinary tile and mouldings were cut and reformed to create the showpiece star design. A palette of natural stone and tile, when juxtaposed, creates an interesting tonal pattern that complements the turquoise swimming pool color. Arch details and sculptural columns made of hand-carved cantera stone add architectural definition.

FACING PAGE: A 12-foot diameter floor design centered in the radius-cut foyer showcases Old World stone workmanship; the combination of Italian Crema Marfil marble, Emperador Dark marble and Giallo Reale work together in a harmonious pattern reminiscent of a circular, hand-woven rug. Stonework designs with such ornate patterns require painstaking attention to detail. We fabricated and installed marble slab steps featuring inlaid designs to reiterate the motif as one ascends the staircase. Our team collaborated with T's Construction on this project.

Photographs courtesy of Picasso Tile & Design

"Natural stone and handmade tiles have been used throughout the ages. We procure rare and beautiful stone from quarries around the world as well as indigenous materials for more environmentally focused projects."

—Michele Kalec

ABOVE: This traditional kitchen in a Paradise Valley residence features a gourmet island food preparation surface and kitchen counters. The entire perimeter of the center island showcases radius-cut granite sides and a special profile that help to soften the large piece.

Photograph by Adam Rodriguez, Adamsphoto

FACING PAGE: Nature's motifs are emphasized in our Hawaiian spa and bath designs. One master bath features mocha and black porcelain tile walls with a dramatic lily design; variegated, brushed granite counters and a minimalist slab vessel complete the look. We created a Zen-inspired master shower area with smooth porcelain tile and hand-chiseled limestone. The combination of tones and textures is a perfect backdrop for the 1,400-pound black granite soaking tub, creating a welcome respite. For a modern interpretation, we integrated glass tile mosaics in the custom shower and bath combined with enduring granite counters. Time-intensive mosaic work was created using glass tiles from Spain and Italy and accented by tumbled, polished byzantine natural stones.

Photographs courtesy of Picasso Tile & Design

AVAI

"Efficient integration. That's where the real power of technology lies."

—Rand Arnold

ABOVE: There's nothing quite as rewarding as bringing together the perfect blend of technology for an estate and making it user-friendly. The numerous systems required to operate a large home aren't necessarily designed to work with each other, but we can integrate anything—from audiovisual and lighting to security, telecommunications, pool temperature, room humidity, motorized blinds, sprinkler systems and more. It's the art of technology. Though everything about the job is complex, our philosophy is simple: Home systems should be intuitive, and they should perform to perfection.
Photograph by Bill Timmerman

FACING PAGE: For a family who wanted to watch a single television from anywhere in the kitchen, living room or adjacent patio without having their prime views of the city interrupted, we came up with the dropdown projection screen solution. The screen is equal parts opaque and transportive, so the picture is crystal clear, albeit reversed when viewed from the kitchen. Our solution-driven process starts and ends with wants and wishes of the people who will benefit from the day-to-day convenience and leisure afforded by the technology.
Photograph by John Trotto

ABOVE: My background is in computer engineering, and many of my colleagues studied computer science, electrical engineering and related technical fields; we're big on efficiency and meticulously documenting our processes, which is why we don't hesitate to take on even the most daunting projects. We like a good challenge, and when you see how expansive the control room of an estate is, it becomes clear why integrating disparate and complex systems is so important. Most homeowners don't want to deal with technology; they want their lives to be seamlessly enhanced by it.
Photograph courtesy of AVAI

FACING PAGE TOP: Putting a television outside was once just a temporary fix—it was only a matter of time before the elements got the best of it. We relish using tried-and-true materials in unexpected ways, so for a homeowner intent on an outdoor television, we used oceanglass—the impervious material that encloses Shamu's underwater environment—as the screen for the rear-lit projection system built right into the side of the house.
Photograph by John Trotto

FACING PAGE BOTTOM: The home's digital interface is amazing. With an intuitive drag-and-drop, touch-screen controller, the residents can choose to simultaneously view any combination of television shows, movies or even security feed and home systems status on the sizeable plasma screen.
Photograph by John Trotto

"People often focus on novel technologies and 'giggle factor' installations. The true challenge, however, is providing a well-planned system with an intuitive interface. When these details are perfected, they enhance everyday life."

—Rand Arnold

ABOVE & FACING PAGE: A homeowner told us that the "brains" of her home was the best part, and we couldn't have said it better. Whether we're doing a technology forward or a technology sublime project, we're focused on creating lifestyles of luxury. We program a couple dozen scene-setting modes for each home so that the owners don't need any sort of learning curve. Fingerprint analysis, reverse caller ID lookup, special access codes for family and staff, quiet intercom announcements as people enter and depart the property, advance notification as the time-of-day mode changes—nothing is out of reach. And to make sure that all systems are in order, we monitor homes around the clock, often notifying owners of problems and solution timeframes before they even realize something's off-line. Reliability and ease of use—that's what advanced home systems are all about.
Photographs by Coles Hairston

BENTWOOD LUXURY KITCHENS

Dallas, Texas — Houston, Texas

"A custom kitchen should ultimately exude the feeling of indulgence."

—Randy Pittard

ABOVE & FACING PAGE: It is important to marry form and function in every kitchen design. Our minimalist kitchen is ultra chic and represents the Urban Loft collection. Solid glass countertops with their natural green tint are harder than granite surfaces, providing durability and lasting performance. Ebony wood cabinetry with frosted glass inserts in the doors creates high drama. The glass tile backsplash has luminous hues of watery blue and light green for a fresh, contemporary effect when juxtaposed with ebony cabinets and stainless steel elements. We believe in customizing kitchens to an extreme through the finest materials, expert craftsmanship and development of new creative concepts.

Photographs by Power Creative

"Luxury in a traditional kitchen must capture the senses with historic character and European nuances."

—Randy Pittard

ABOVE: We designed refined cabinetry reminiscent of the late 1700s based on woodwork styles from the period and recreated its French historic look. We chose our hand-applied cream-colored finish for the butler's pantry with its X-patterned window framework and diamond-shaped bas relief panels. Adjacent cabinetry features a subdued basil green finish in both the utility room and scullery for European authenticity. Our French Country collection possesses the finest Old World joinery and finishing methods.

ABOVE & FACING PAGE: We created a classical kitchen using richly hand-painted black cabinetry with gold and red antiqued highlights; the world-class kitchen was distinguished for its elegance and dimensional pyramid design on the doors. Pure white Carerra marble used on the oven surround and island surface combines with sleek stainless steel countertops to give sharp contrast against the midnight black finish. We attached two reclaimed, unfinished antique doors from the mid-1800s for a genuine French accent. The sophisticated traditional kitchen is part of our prestigious Jack Arnold designer collection.

Photographs by Hawks Photography

"Beautiful kitchens begin with a seed of inspiration."

—Randy Pittard

ABOVE LEFT & RIGHT: Enchanting English-style cabinets from our Classics collection are hand-painted with a timeworn finish in lichen tones. We designed traditional mullion doors with a beautiful laser-cut rose pattern on the lower doors, which is also mirrored in the water-etched roses of the marble oven surround. The adjoining butler's pantry with its center island dons a slightly golden chablis finish.

Photographs by Power Creative

FACING PAGE: Whether designing in a traditional, transitional or modern style, we use quality materials in manufacturing, as the final fabrication reflects the good taste of those who dwell within. Our riftsawn white oak cabinetry with its distinctive grain has a soy finish and is from our Pacific Rim collection. Polished marble counters with dark cabinetry give a hint of tradition in the open kitchen layout. We created a genuine teakwood surround to add interest around the oven for a striking combination of wood grains that exude true luxury.

Photographs by Cabinetry Creations

LMC Home Entertainment

"State-of-the-art systems allow residents to experience the full impact of Hollywood's finest productions. We create spaces that transport people wherever their imagination takes them."

—Mike Ware

ABOVE & FACING PAGE: We created a home theater featuring a 12-foot-wide Stewart Cinemascope screen and 9.4 surround sound for movie presentations that surpass the local cinema. High definition, crisp colors, amazing surround sound and accent lighting are all part of our holistic design approach. We designed a three-dimensional starlit sky indoors: Fiber optic "star" strands of different diameters and lengths are suspended above the soffit to create a magical experience. Sconce lighting, millwork built by our resident cabinet-maker, acoustical materials on walls with rich fabric coverings, high-end European carpet and custom seating add to the luxurious ambience. Classical columns hold surround sound speakers, and crescent-patterned fabric carries the Art Deco-inspired theme.
Photographs by Neal Hightower

"Legendary music and cinema starts with the finest American- and European-built components and ends with great millwork and furnishings. Every design element must be integrated flawlessly."

—Mike Ware

LEFT: The small-scale room is packed with power. We installed an eight-foot-wide screen for optimal viewing with high-end McIntosh equipment into a flush-mounted sliding rack and audiophile-approved Sonus Faber speakers from Italy, offering the emotional excitement of a pure musical event. Our design features fabric-covered wall panels concealing custom-acoustical treatments. Theater-style seating and custom alder wood trim adds a dramatic feeling to the intimate space. We often collaborate with architects, builders and interior designers, elevating the vision to create the total sensory environment.

FACING PAGE TOP: We mounted high-end McIntosh components into a slab of royal red granite. The custom unit is flanked by unique columns that house rear surround speakers behind 1920s Art Deco-inspired grill cloth; the wooden structures in front of each column are made of individual slats of alder wood designed to act as acoustical diffusers. The complex home theater system looks intimidating but is easy to use with the single touch of a control panel or iPhone.

FACING PAGE BOTTOM: Savant's futuristic touchscreen panels work like an iPod for complete fingertip control. Each visual is designed to depict an actual room in the house. The user-friendly automated system allows residents to merely touch drapery, lamps or shades to activate and control functions.
Photographs by Neal Hightower

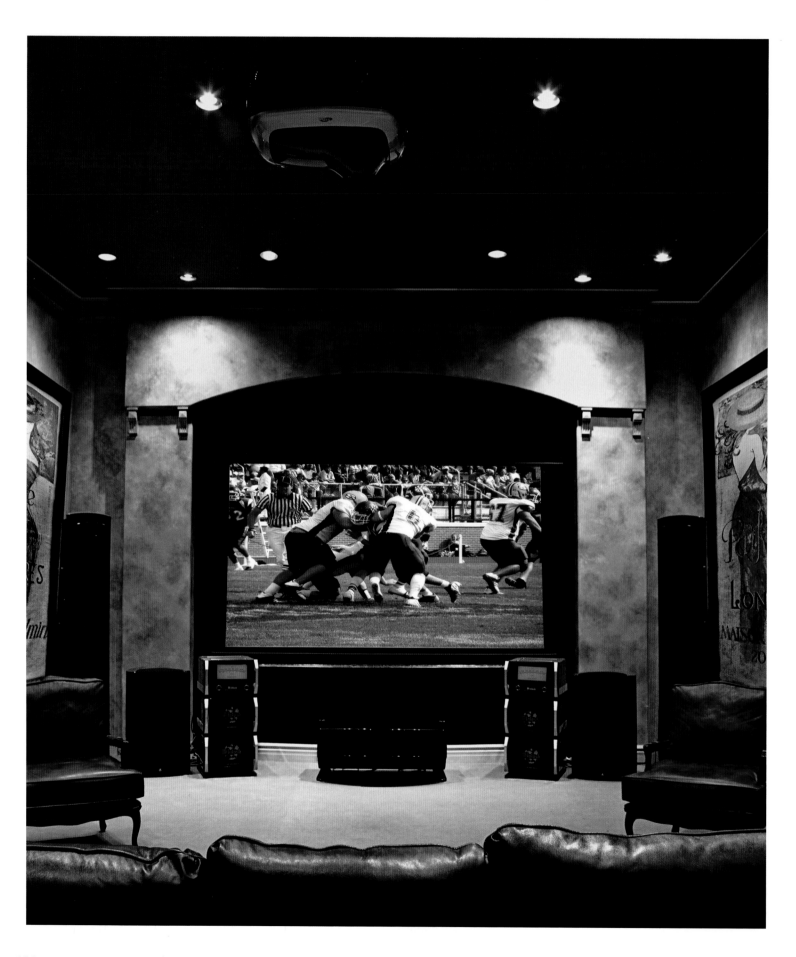

"We feature world-class brands—exclusive audio and video products designed and built in the United States, Europe and Japan—for the ultimate musical and theatrical sound experience."

—Mike Ware

ABOVE: Our German-engineered MBL Luxury Line is the epitome of an uber-speaker concept that is unparalleled worldwide—the MBL 101 Radialstrahler X-Treme. It is the most advanced music system on the planet, reflective of the three months it takes to assemble and calibrate. As the exclusive MBL X-Treme dealer for North America, we design and install the coveted $250,000 speakers reserved for music aficionados who expect exceptional sound quality.
Photograph by Neal Hightower

FACING PAGE: We designed the ultimate "man cave" that includes seven-foot-tall McIntosh tower speakers and Monoblock amplifiers along with a pair of J.L. Gotham subwoofers; the total system's power is an amazing 38,600 watts. An impressive drop-down screen is ideal for sports viewing: the state-of-the-art 135-inch screen delivers live action as if you were at the event. Our seating area rests on a full-motion platform that moves with up to 2 g-force, choreographed to movies, sporting events or video games. We also created the room's faux finish and custom millwork for a neoclassic element with framed tapestries on side walls for a touch of Old World tradition.
Photograph by Sean Shelton

PAUL J. LABADIE CRAFTSMAN COMPANY

Dallas, Texas

"Traditional Japanese apprentice carpenters swear an oath to their masters to never end the life of a tree but to extend it through their work; I admire that spirit of honor and dignity and am inspired by it."

—Paul J. Labadie

ABOVE: The ornate tracery's volutes and leafy flourishes with egg-and-dart cornice mouldings in the entablature were painstakingly handcrafted. I made the bookcase cabinet doors with diamond-patterned leaded glass the traditional way with pegged-through, mortise-and-tenon joinery. In the frieze above the tracery, there are alternating medallions of lion heads and family crest shields.

FACING PAGE: This stately residence's private study was intended to hold the homeowner's treasured library collection. We aspired to create a special room for theological books that was evocative of a majestic and sacred atmosphere. The ornamental scheme for the study is an original design based on historic examples of the Venetian Gothic style. Walls are paneled in bookmatched walnut veneer, and custom handcarved woodwork is crafted of solid walnut hardwood. Tracery and other embellishments were handcarved after a pattern inspired by intricate 15th-century stonework façades on Venice's Grand Canal.
Photographs by Dan Sellers

"A room, a piece of furniture or a house should possess a beautiful overall effect but also have proportional details that harmonize with each other and resonate with the whole."

—Paul J. Labadie

RIGHT: The library boasts 12-foot ceilings with a central dome ascending to 18 feet tall at its central point. This design was conceived, in keeping with the Gothic style, to accentuate the verticality of the space. The concentration of ornament above the paneling and bookcases leads the eye upward to the lettered entablature at the base of the dome all the way to the top. I designed and fabricated every woodwork component in my studio then assembled and installed them into the room. After installation, the handcarved raw walnut hardwood pieces were lightly stained and varnished to bring out their natural grain and unify wood tones. The design phase involves collaboration with the architect, homeowner and builder, and final installation requires coordination with contractors. My personal attention is given to every aspect from concept stage to project completion.

Photograph by Dan Sellers

"I don't try to carve ornaments perfectly; technology can do that, and the effect is lifeless. The human element makes handwork better than perfect."

—Paul J. Labadie

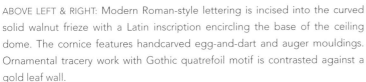

ABOVE LEFT & RIGHT: Modern Roman-style lettering is incised into the curved solid walnut frieze with a Latin inscription encircling the base of the ceiling dome. The cornice features handcarved egg-and-dart and auger mouldings. Ornamental tracery work with Gothic quatrefoil motif is contrasted against a gold leaf wall.

FACING PAGE TOP: Tucked into the triangular spaces of the tracery are 28 hand-carved cherubs. The gilded figurines are each unique and hold crimson-painted wooden ribbons with the words of a favorite *Bible* verse. I carved the cherubs using miniature hand tools and gilded them before assembling into the tracery.

FACING PAGE BOTTOM: I have a passion for creating original designs in historic styles using authentic traditional methods that have stood the test of time. My carving chisels, gouges and mallets are no different than those used by carvers hundreds of years ago. Refined detail is my specialty; I carved ornamental seraphim and incorporated one at the bottom of each vertical tracery piece as a finishing touch.

Photographs by Dan Sellers

"All floors are not created equal. Custom wood floors provide distinctive looks for both contemporary and traditional interiors."

—Greg Schenck

ABOVE: The handsome study features a semi-circular credenza. In keeping with the graceful lines, we created a border by bending planks to follow the radius of the curve. Our rich and elegant basketweave pattern consists of hand-scraped hickory with walnut inserts. Artisans scraped wood planks prior to installation, but the wood flooring was hand-stained and finished on site.

FACING PAGE: A contemporary space is further defined by domestic maple flooring that has been rift and quartered to minimize grain. The lack of grain and neutral palette provides a perfect canvas for furniture, fine art and accessories. We installed the flooring in a traditional herringbone pattern with a simple border, allowing the wood's natural hues to emerge. The protective, low-sheen, non-ambering finish creates a soft, soothing environment.
Photographs by Steve Chenn

"Wood flooring should not be the hero of a space. It should fit seamlessly into the overall design theme of a home."

—Greg Schenck

LEFT: A Houston penthouse owner procured antique flooring reclaimed from a London structure for use in his new high-rise home. We re-milled the centuries-old pieces and cut planks to form a unique herringbone floor pattern. Our craftsmen hand-scraped and refinished the wood for additional character. Reclaimed wood lends an Old World charm to an otherwise modern space. We often source salvaged timber to create floors that are environmentally friendly as well as attractive.

FACING PAGE TOP: Reclaimed longleaf pine—with original saw marks more than 100 years old—gives character and texture to the lodge-like trophy room. This increasingly rare American wood is no longer commercially harvested. We re-milled the back surface but allowed the aged and weathered "face" to remain intact then hand-applied multiple coats of burnished oil to seal the wood, giving it a fine furniture finish with a stain-free, natural patina.

FACING PAGE BOTTOM: A rich, paneled library features a stone-and-wood flooring design. The hand-scraped walnut planks define the elevation and create the dramatic frame for the inlaid antique stone. The challenge was to seamlessly transition the tile and wood.
Photographs by Steve Chenn

"The moment you enter a room, hardwood floors set the tone. The subtle details of the wood should help define the interior ambience."

—Greg Schenck

ABOVE: Our timeless flooring design suits the well-established residence. We added warmth and a hint of age to new American cherry wood flooring by creating hand-beveled edges and gentle wear patterns. Multiple woods were used to fashion curved inlays, the border and the classic herringbone pattern that creates a unique statement and enhances the gracious flow of the room's architecture.

FACING PAGE: We worked closely with the interior designer to reflect the architecture of the vaulted ceilings in our flooring design for the gallery. Utilizing an oversized herringbone pattern in hand-scraped hickory, we transformed the long, narrow space into a series of smaller, more intimate vestibules.
Photographs by Steve Chenn

ACCENT DESIGN AND MANUFACTURING

"A custom staircase should enhance the beauty of a home's interior and create an inviting focal point."

—Murray Herron

ABOVE & FACING PAGE: Distinctive stairways can encompass a range of structural styles, including freestanding, curved, spiral and winding or precisely straight and angular to integrate with the established architecture of a home. We fabricate unique traditional and contemporary staircases, balconies, gates and fencing; our handcrafted design elements are meant to complement an interior or exterior theme. Homeowners may be inspired by a favorite childhood residence or travels to enchanting European castles; we take this information and create a custom piece designed with sophisticated form and function. By following the design philosophy of "less is more," the nuances of an architectural style are best expressed.
Above photograph courtesy of Accent Design and Mfg.
Facing page photograph by Mark Boisclair

"It takes the talent of a true artisan to create highly personalized style, whether the look is contemporary or classical, masculine or feminine."

—Cathy Herron

RIGHT & FACING PAGE: Engineered stair systems, such as "floating" staircases—with cantilevered structural landings that don't need newel posts for visual appeal—can transform a home from ordinary to extraordinary. Wrought iron, hardwood, sleek glass and strong metals are the best mediums for fabricating timeless staircases. Our creations blend imported pieces made using Old World techniques with modern railings and treads; we often combine ornate ironwork and handsome millwork to make a sophisticated statement. An incredible custom stairway is like a beautiful sculpture. Final finishes are as important as the design and structural integrity to achieve a luxurious look.

Right photograph by Robert Reck
Facing page photographs courtesy of Accent Design and Mfg.

"The beauty in working with metal is creating pieces that read well from afar and up close."

—Oleg Shyshkin

ABOVE: I have a special understanding of how art and structure should integrate. In my native Ukraine, I worked on incredible projects like the restoration of the Old City part of Kiev. I've practiced architecture and explored painting, interior design and a variety of other creative mediums, which help me excel in my true passion: blacksmithing. No other technique can transform lines into art as well as wrought iron—if I can sketch it on paper, I can forge it in metal.

FACING PAGE: Everything I do is an original design. I am very close to my work and will often linger on projects in their final stages simply because I want to continue working on them. I had the opportunity to create an elaborate entry gate for an Eastern European client's Ontario countryside estate. Drawing inspiration from songs about the moon and local terrain that I heard in my youth, I designed the 22-foot-wide central piece to be very connected with nature.
Photographs by Oleg Shyshkin

> "Blacksmithing is an intuitive process that requires a great deal of physical work and even more creativity and patience."

—Oleg Shyshkin

RIGHT: Wrought iron is a graphic material with infinite possibilities. I've always been fascinated by the variety of mailboxes in this world. They are such focal points that they really should be more aesthetically engaging. I designed and forged one for a good friend of mine who is a fisherman. I chose a nautical theme and ornamented the post with animated sea creatures. Now I have a full collection of one-of-a-kind mailboxes.

FACING PAGE TOP LEFT: The tools of my craft are eternal. With my hammer and anvil, I use iron, water, air and fire; the concepts of my creations are equally organic. For a private wine cellar, I designed the stair rail to emerge from the floor like a vine. The young branches grow toward the light, twisting with each other and ultimately producing clusters of grapes—the 150-plus grapes are individually forged. I engineered the piece to stand securely with only seven screws, giving it a light feel despite the heaviness of the material.

FACING PAGE TOP RIGHT: A couple came to me wanting a simple wine cooler with candelabra element for their master bathing suite. The site-specific piece adds a romantic, luxuriously custom quality to the space. All of my work blends a love of French Art Nouveau with American Art Deco; the aesthetic is very unique.

FACING PAGE BOTTOM: People's eyes naturally focus on what's there rather than what's not. The traditional elements missing from my 150-foot serpentine railing are posts and legs. I wanted the design to be light and elegant, not overpowered by weighty vertical bars. Pieces this large often take years to complete even when I have other metalworkers assisting me with the fabrication. It is a tremendous honor to know that the fruits of my labor are enjoyed from Dallas to Vladivostok.

Photographs by Oleg Shyshkin

"Achieving the perfect balance of beauty and function requires a vivid imagination and a process that begins with understanding how the space will be used."

—Mary Calvin

ABOVE: As an exclusive Wood-Mode Lifestyle Design Showroom offering Wood-Mode and Brookhaven fine custom cabinetry, we specialize in creating distinctive kitchens for discerning homeowners. Commissioned to transform a small kitchen into a spacious gathering place, we gave the beautiful natural cherry wood cabinets a black glaze finish that will develop a rich patina over time.

FACING PAGE: Mitered traditional cabinet doors are topped with matching cherry wood crown mouldings to create a warm and inviting ambience. Our fresh ideas coupled with Wood-Mode's quality products allow for a multitude of design expressions.

Photographs by Anthony Rathbun

"Everyone wants a beautiful kitchen, but a successful design must first consider functionality. We strive to marry form and function."

—Mary Calvin

ABOVE: A beach house kitchen mirrors the family's lifestyle. We created a custom color of coastal blue for the maple cabinets; glass inserts showcase a sea coral collection. Our design includes refrigerator panels and the decorative range hood with a display shelf, valance and beadboard paneling.
Photograph by Sylvester Garza

FACING PAGE TOP LEFT: The custom cherry wood veneer cabinetry has a contemporary look. Frosted glass panels in upper cabinets flank the stove with its built-in appliances.
Photograph courtesy of Cabinet Innovations

FACING PAGE TOP RIGHT: Aluminum framed doors with acid-etched glass are housed in dark cherry cabinetry to further define a sleek design yet exude a warm feeling.
Photograph by Anthony Rathbun

FACING PAGE BOTTOM LEFT: Cherry wood cabinetry is glazed, distressed and burnished to resemble freestanding antique furniture. We designed the hand-carved hood covered in limestone and added crown moulding for Old World character.
Photograph by Sylvester Garza

FACING PAGE BOTTOM RIGHT: Our transitional interpretation of a maple kitchen provides a spacious, child-friendly environment. Classic display cabinets, carved corbels and a clever appliance garage are uncommon details.
Photograph by Rick Gardner

GARCIA ART GLASS

"Once a vision is established, I use my artistic language and aesthetic interpretation to bring the molten glass to life for a specific environment."

—Gini Garcia

ABOVE & FACING PAGE: As an industrial designer who studied glass blowing in Maine, New York and Louisiana and chandelier-making in Murano, Italy, I deeply understand that working with this living medium is about integrating form, color and texture to create a relationship with light. My chandeliers and hanging sculptures often involve making a series of small pieces out of molten glass. They are gathered from the furnace, cooled, then wired to a welded armature and electrified from inside. Working as the vehicle for visualizing concepts, I let the client, situation or environment present itself to me. In turn, I respond with ideas for the missing piece of inspiration. Whether people are looking at vibrant, multicolored or monochromatic chandeliers, the texture draws you closer to view the exquisite interplay of light and shadow.

Photographs by Greg Harrison

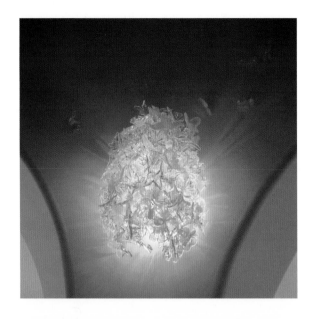

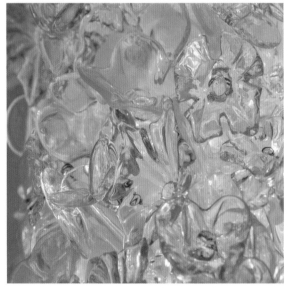

"Hand-blown glass chandeliers, vessels and sculpture become filters for light, magically reflecting shadows and shapes all around the room."

—Gini Garcia

LEFT: One art collector-homeowner had an affinity for butterflies. My research involved observation of the annual monarch butterfly migration in Mexico, and then I recreated the fragile winged creatures out of clear blown glass to catch nuances of color. Four ethereal 24-inch sconces were covered with dozens of delicate glass butterflies; our team attached 148 single butterflies to appear as though they were fluttering up the walls to the domed ceiling. We painstakingly install every unique art glass commission on location.
Top & bottom photographs by Greg Harrison
Middle photograph by G3 Advanced

FACING PAGE: Fiery forms, flower shapes and organic ribbons of hand-blown glass are feature elements for some of my breathtaking chandeliers and dramatic sculptures. I am forever inspired by the classical still life paintings of the 16th century where the subject matter of abundance and opulence is evident. I work to create glass pieces that resemble nature's array of exotic fruits such as cacao and pomegranate pods. Each fantasy art glass creation becomes a vibrant celebration of forms and hangs like brilliant "jewelry" in the home.
Top & bottom left photographs by Greg Harrison
Top & bottom right photographs by G3 Advanced

"A muralist must consider the whole space when designing the work of art."

—Gillian Bradshaw-Smith

ABOVE: For the historical home's foyer, I painted a Tuscan landscape in situ. As a person descends the stairs, the painted landscape transitions with grace from the sky to the ground-floor garden terrace. A faux stone garden wall supports the stairway. I added a shaded blue sky high above the Italian countryside; the family's white kitty and golden retriever also appear in the pastoral setting. Pedestals flank a door, and decorative architectural details exhibit a touch of trompe l'oeil technique.
Photograph by Gillian Bradshaw-Smith

FACING PAGE: I created a hunting-inspired landscape using stylized realism; the painting depicts a traditional fox hunt. The complete mural flows from scene to scene around the room. Horses gallop along a stream with the hounds running in pursuit of a red fox while a stag stands alone on the hill above a rock formation. I brushed and sponged thinned latex and acrylic paints onto primed muslin in the studio then applied the large-scale finished paintings to wall sections for a seamless fit.
Photograph by Jag Gonzalez

"Decorative, faux and illusion paintings can transform a room into something special."

—Gillian Bradshaw-Smith

RIGHT: Through traditional painting in the ancient decorative style of Portuguese azulejos, I created a terracotta tile mural. Hand-painted decorative Venetian dolphins, flowers and architectural details add structure to the design by use of a limited palette of ochre pigments. Our tile maker then glazed and fired them, ready to install as a custom wainscot for an elegant kitchen. I often collaborate with interior designer Barry Williams.
Photograph by Barry Williams

FACING PAGE: Art from all periods has become inspiration for many of my murals. The paneled living room ceiling concept was inspired by the Roman art of Pompeii. I painted the mural on muslin panels that were first coated with fine plaster then after completion distressed the paintings to look like they rose from the ashes of ruins. For a final touch, I accented the painting's details and wood mouldings with genuine white gold leaf. On some wall murals, I strive to portray the beauty of nature using the Chinese style, capturing a plant or a creature's vividness in a few simple yet masterful brushstrokes.
Photographs by Dan Doughty

MORRISON SUPPLY COMPANY

"Plumbing fixtures, lighting, appliances and hardware are the jewelry of the home."

—Scott Sangalli

ABOVE: Accessorizing a room with the right fixtures, appliances and hardware can be a time consuming and daunting project if not addressed properly. The process is greatly streamlined if selections can be accomplished in a setting where all elements are chosen and viewed simultaneously. Every detail matters. In our master bath, the Kohler Kallista fixtures include an architecturally inspired pedestal sink, toilet and faucets, generous whirlpool tub and decorative towel bars. Discriminating homeowners understand and embrace a unified approach to design.

FACING PAGE: The kitchen, being the heart of the home, has become the most popular room where family and friends frequently gather, thus compelling buyers to attain a kitchen that is designed to include much more than the original function. Ultimately it should be beautiful, inviting and useful. It should balance flow and maximize the utilization of space. Properly done, the kitchen will create an engaging ambience for food prep as well as entertaining.
Photographs by Sylvester Garza

"Our impressions and perceptions are the result of what we see as well as what we touch and feel. What we feel should never contradict what we see."

—Scott Sangalli

LEFT: Delighting the senses is the aesthetic goal when designing the dwelling's exterior façade as well as its intimate interior. The entrance to a home should project a warm, welcoming invitation while reflecting a feeling of substance and security. Foremost a home should proudly stand in its beauty and appeal, prompting intrigue to both visitors and passersby alike.
Photograph by Lindsay Marie De Marco

FACING PAGE TOP: Proper balance, proportion, scale, massing, functionality and material selection are the requisites of superior design. Our model kitchen incorporates a variety of finishes and materials: natural stone, painted and distressed woods, stucco, clay tile, artisan iron, glass, stainless steel, brushed metals and ceramics.
Photograph by George Gutenberg

FACING PAGE BOTTOM: We advise choosing the finest hardware that the budget will allow. Today's vast selections are available in traditional and contemporary designs with a range of sophisticated finishes. The wide variety of products from quality manufacturers permits homeowners to express personal style while maintaining visual harmony with the residence's distinctive character and architectural form.
Photographs by Lindsay Marie De Marco

PALMER TODD

Austin, Texas — San Antonio, Texas

"It's imperative that a kitchen's design match the architecture of the home—nothing should look out of place."

—Christi Palmer

ABOVE: Simplicity and bold colors make spaces come alive. We incorporated a homeowner's love of vibrant colors without overpowering the room. Three basic finishes—red, stainless steel and light wood tone—capture the home's style and reveal the residents' taste. The kitchen lacks traditional adornment—such as corbels, crown mouldings and stacked columns—and instead shows off strong design. Because the homeowners also use the space as a test kitchen for their food preparation business, functionality became even more important. Wide, open countertops, duplicate appliances and plenty of storage make the kitchen work on a professional level.

FACING PAGE: Symmetrically oriented with the home's architecture, the kitchen maintains a subtle, understated beauty. The island serves multiple purposes: The raised section offers much-needed storage and provides a visual barrier between guests and the workspace while the three-sided lower section supplies extra counter space. Simple yet eye-catching, the pendant lights direct sightlines into the kitchen. Features like lightly glazed cabinets with Carrera marble countertops and rich walnut floors give the space its overall elegance.
Photographs by Tre Dunham, Fine Focus Photography

"Don't overcrowd a space. Clean lines create stunning kitchens."

—Christi Palmer

ABOVE: Achieving a kitchen with Asian simplicity and Southwestern flair took an artist's touch. Sliding screens with lacquer inserts trimmed with dark Nubian oak panels conceal valuable storage space and offer strong lines. The granite island adds a warm color palette to accent the space.
Photograph by Tre Dunham, Fine Focus Photography

FACING PAGE TOP: Some kitchens demand two islands. For a home with vast expanses, one island was designed to serve as a complete work station. Its proximity to the range and inclusion of a sink, dishwasher and surface space made it ideal for this purpose. The second island functions as a serving area and cocktail space with refrigerated drawers and an icemaker.
Photograph courtesy of Bravo Interior Design

FACING PAGE BOTTOM: For a homeowner who wanted a bright, open feel without sacrificing an ounce of comfort, we used a mixture of finishes and materials.
Photograph by Tre Dunham, Fine Focus Photography

"For the same reason it doesn't take a trained chef to appreciate a good meal, it doesn't take an audiologist to recognize the best theater sound. Everyone can enjoy our work."

—Russ Berger

ABOVE: Getting inside of homeowners' heads to understand their lifestyles is the best way to get great results. For a music-loving family, we created a living area that doubles as a piano room—perfect for impromptu playing. An attached game room adds to the fun.

FACING PAGE: For a sleek and modern home theater, we broke with design convention to deliver bold results. Pure white walls typically won't work in a screening area since they reflect light, both from the screen and the window. The solution: Blackout shades and sliding panels emerge from hidden recesses to control light, making the stunning aesthetics possible. Matching the home's vocabulary, the space lends itself to hanging out in style.
Photographs © rbdg.com

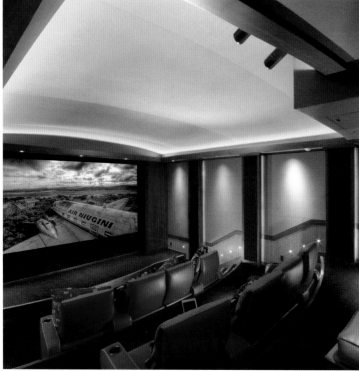

"We began by developing solutions for hundreds of THX, United Artists, General Cinema, AMC Theaters and Cinemark. Our home screening room environments give residents every reason to skip the traditional theater experience."

—Russ Berger

RIGHT: Our work reflects architecture, interior design and technology. A gently sloped hallway smoothly transitions from the home into the theater. The décor brings all of the elements together, from stylish theater posters to lighting fixtures found elsewhere in the home.

FACING PAGE TOP: When the screen goes up and the speakers tuck into the walls, a view of Lake Michigan appears. Set in a downtown penthouse, the theater has proven itself a sound investment for the residents with the promise of providing years of enjoyment for family and friends. Media is one of life's greatest pleasures.

FACING PAGE BOTTOM LEFT: Grab a bag of popcorn or a bottle of wine and turn down the lights—everyone has fun at the cinema. For a family with two children, we included a stage at the front and a crow's nest in the back for the ultimate theater. While children use the stage space to perform, adults can hold a comfortable conference. Excellent acoustics, attractive aesthetics, appropriate seating and a well-planned room configuration make for an ideal executive home theater.

FACING PAGE BOTTOM RIGHT: Benches on the side of the room and meal-friendly seating give an unconventional feel to a home theater. Meeting the family's needs is the most important consideration when designing an audiovisual space, whether it is completely eccentric or a traditional-style theater.
Photographs © rbdg.com

SIGMA MARBLE GRANITE AND TILE

Dallas, Texas

"There is nothing comparable to the beauty of natural stone."

—George Kanaan

ABOVE: Durable Brazilian granite on the vanity and shower walls of a master bath exudes a spa-like ambience. We installed yellow-hued Giallo Veneziano granite tiles with a contrasting black granite decorative border. Granite was chosen over marble because, while both have the same density, polished granite better retains its shine and withstands water and weathering in bathrooms and kitchens. As true artisans of natural stone, we can fabricate and re-form slabs, rough blocks and tiles to fit any interior design.

FACING PAGE: We imported classic French hauteville limestone with an overall taupe color; its rust and burgundy-veined character creates an impressive and elegant foyer. The thermal "flamed" finish also provides a slightly textured surface. To achieve a custom luxury look, we shape prestigious natural stone varieties in our shop according to the builder's specifications. Our forte is applying the latest technology and innovations in stone-cutting and installation; the results are stunning.
Photographs by DVD Design Group, Inc.

"To create a perfect installation, one must understand the design intent and keep the vision throughout the process."

—George Kanaan

RIGHT: Historically used in palaces and homes of nobility, natural artisan stone, whether polished, honed or thermally treated, stands the test of time in formal rooms or casual living spaces.

FACING PAGE: Any interior or exterior aesthetic—rustic chic, clean contemporary or regal sophistication—can be achieved through the versatility and enduring quality of marble and other natural stone selections. We cut and shape some of the hardest materials on earth. Our artisans apply ancient mosaic techniques, carve special details and create finishing trims to frame flooring, walls and architectural elements.

Photographs by DVD Design Group, Inc.

WOODWRIGHT HARDWOOD FLOOR COMPANY

Dallas, Texas

"It takes both true craftsmanship and technological innovation to achieve an enduring work of art."

—Steve Welch

ABOVE: The exceptional living room features plainsawn North American walnut presented in the elegant Versailles pattern. Rare figured and burled walnut center squares add texture and interest. The floor's perimeter features book-matched fancy and burled walnut planks, which were sliced in half and then folded over to mirror grain patterns and match the edges. We manufacture custom hardwood floors beginning with a choice of raw lumber to creating laser-cut shapes for intricate patterns and details.

FACING PAGE: A penthouse rotunda foyer showcases dark walnut planking with a rich mahogany outer circle and Wenge inner stripe. The round, fan-shaped radial design is crafted of burled walnut for a stunning textural effect. We integrated hardwood pieces with natural stone so that walking across the floor is one even level. The result is a beautiful and seamless surface.
Photographs by Steve Welch

"Science and art should intertwine. An understanding of hardwood species, how they react to environmental conditions, is essential."

—Steve Welch

TOP: The private condo has a decidedly contemporary feel, and our wide carbonized bamboo plank floor with its well-defined grain completes the look. Each plank is finished with a cobblestone surface treatment to soften edges with a shadow line. We believe in being eco-sensitive and, whenever possible, use renewable resources and wood derived from managed forests.
Photograph by John Davis

BOTTOM: Artistically arranged riftsawn and quartersawn red oak planks on stairs and landings create continuity of design in the home while providing lasting wear for years of enjoyment. Riftsawn planks are cut from lumber on an angle at the edge of a tree's growth rings to create a more stable piece of wood yet maintain a uniform grain pattern among different boards.
Photograph by Steve Welch

FACING PAGE: Exquisite flooring is only limited by the imagination of the homeowner or designer. We execute the most complex designs utilizing state-of-the-art technology and proper installation techniques. Our creative flooring designs display unique contrast and visual appeal. We select hardwood species that possess color differentiation in their natural state and will accept the same depth of color when stained. We can meet unique flooring requests such as combining wood pieces with leather for an exotic, one-of-a-kind effect that is soft underfoot. Our skillful craftsmen are adept at recreating any desired design from basketweave patterns to classic Greek key borders and contemporary, stylized designs with hand inlaid pieces, meticulously arranged to form logos and highly tailored motifs.
Photographs by Steve Welch

"Natural stone adds enduring beauty to a home. Every piece of stone has a story to tell from the depths of the earth, displaying unique color and personality."

—Arturo Pedroza

ABOVE LEFT & MIDDLE: Cantera stone is a strong, malleable rock of volcanic origin that comes in a broad spectrum of colors, mainly imported from Mexico and Central America. We created spiral columns with Corinthian capitals and classical balustrades for a Greek-inspired residential design. Impressive café galindo columns with an elegant, hand-carved Mayan motif delineate the façade.
Photographs courtesy of Columns Design

ABOVE RIGHT: Madera cantera stone has the color tones and variegated pattern of wood grain. We hand-carved Tuscan columns for a luxurious bathroom spa to create an authentic Roman bath ambience. Cantera stone is our specialty, but we have been commissioned to create columns, mouldings and window and fireplace surrounds in natural travertine, shellstone, granite and cast stone.
Photograph courtesy of Columns Design

FACING PAGE: We created exterior Tuscan columns, an archway, the keystone and window surrounds fabricated from large quarried pieces. Our artisans hand-carved each element based on the architect's drawings. We have the ability to recreate any design imaginable; the café galindo cantera stone fountain features realistic royal palms as the sculptural centerpiece.
Photograph by Veronica Luna

"Imported stones from Peru and Israel are superior in performance and beauty, perfectly suited for interior and exterior designs."

—Art Fano

ABOVE: We sourced coral reef Israeli limestone with its naturally embedded seashells for the stunning master bath flooring. The luxury spa walls and vaulted ceilings are lined in a complementary desert taupe selection for a warm glow; small fossils in the limestone create an interesting effect. To achieve the desired architectural definition of the swimming pool hardscape, we integrated solid travertine columns. We import imperial Peruvian travertine with a tempera finish for decks and coping to create a textural surface ideal for poolside safety. The highly versatile and durable stone absorbs less moisture and also resists saltwater weathering.
Left photograph by Bruce Glass
Right photograph courtesy of Jane Page Design Group

FACING PAGE: The impressive foyer and winding stairway treads are crafted using the pinnacle of stones: honed Peruvian travertine from the Andes Mountains. We import 18-inch tiles of richly variegated Crema Viejo for many luxury home projects; the dense, smooth and virtually hole-free nature of the travertine formed in high altitudes allows slabs to be cut thinner, thus the durable stone weighs less. Polished mosaics face the fountain base and stair risers for an artistic touch.
Photograph courtesy of Termeer Custom Homes, LLC

"It always fascinates me to see people's tastes change over the course of a project. The more I expose them to, the more defined and refined their tastes and sense of style become."

—Judy Fox

elements of design

chapter four

Hailing from Massachusetts but a proud longtime resident of Arizona, interior designer Judy Fox savors the opportunity to expand a client's world of design possibilities. She enjoys thoughtfully selecting and presenting a wide array of options so that clients need only focus on their aesthetic preferences. Judy acts as a creative director and a steward of clients' design finances, ensuring that they expend resources in the most meaningful manner. Judy empowers her clients to make well-informed decisions that lead to timeless results; should their ideas differ from her own, she excels at firmly yet politely making her professional recommendations and then graciously proceeding as they wish.

Just as Judy expands her clients' range of knowledge, they expand hers through unique requests; she loves the creative process because everyone grows. By the time clients are ready for a custom home, they've often collected and inherited a lifetime of eclectic treasures. It's Judy's mission to incorporate clients' favorite elements in a thoughtful and unexpected way—blending small-scale furniture into large spaces, for example. Judy is ever mindful of bringing out the best in her clients' cherished pieces as well as the architecture and site. Her relationship-based approach ensures that the interior design of each home is as unique as the people who inhabit it.

JUDY FOX INTERIORS

"If you're planning to remodel, don't try to live in a construction zone. Just move out for a little while and think of your time away as a special vacation."

—Judy Fox

RIGHT: Located north of Scottsdale, the home is nestled into significant acreage—the property line extends into the mountains, allowing homeowners to hike in their backyard. The patio has a nice radius to it and perfectly accommodates the conversational arrangement of cushiony chairs, all of which have great views. The area is tasteful yet has a definite kick-your-feet-up sensibility.

PREVIOUS PAGES: When I was commissioned for the extensive remodel, I knew immediately that the most important element of the whole project would be creating an interior setting that could hold its own with the richness of the natural backdrop. Making the most of the architectural bones and exaggerating the room's proportions, I specified vertical striped floor-to-ceiling silk draperies and a large hand-woven wool rug with an ideally scaled pattern. Rug selection is a lot of fun because I have a number of options shipped in so that my clients and I can see them in place—there's always a standout, and sometimes it surprises. Throughout the home, terracotta and sand tones are combined with dark wood accents; everything has a slightly different distressed finish, which ensures a look that declares it wasn't born yesterday. I designed the bookcase because the room required a piece with very specific dimensions and a unique finish: The burn-through process we used allows the warmth of the natural wood to come through the black varnish; the back wall and shelves are softly glazed so the piece feels light.
Photographs by Karen Shell

"You don't have to agree, but you always have to come to an agreement. Differing perspectives enrich the design journey."

—Judy Fox

ABOVE: Sometimes interior design is about finding a compromise without either party feeling like they've given in. Because the woman of the house was not fond of her husband's rather large LeRoy Neiman painting, the pool room—his lair—became the perfect place for it. I built the paneling and moulding around the piece, whose colors are even more brilliant against the dark wood. We gave the pool table a custom terracotta-colored top to echo the painting and relate to the floor tiles.

FACING PAGE: The breakfast nook's wonderful ceiling is comprised of vegas, thick pine beams that support latillas, smaller beams made from cactus skeletons. The effect is authentically Southwestern, especially in concert with the plastered walls, rounded corners, wrought-iron chandelier and peeled pine poles that flank the space.

Photographs by Karen Shell

"The best projects are those with great clients, a talented team and interesting parameters."

—Judy Fox

ABOVE LEFT: I had hardware custom made to match the mahogany cabinets' scale and depth of color.

ABOVE RIGHT: The entryway offers a taste of the architectural and interior design flavor found throughout the home.

FACING PAGE: I designed the family room sectional expressly for the setting: It perfectly fits the radius of the room and the upholstery is fade-resistant, a necessity with those walls of glass. When I layer a room, I begin with a simple, clean look and then incorporate elements with complex patterns, colors and textures for interest: The throw pillows are like little jewels. I chose two smaller coffee tables that, together, are proportionately appropriate for the room but offer flexibility in placement—people can easily slip between them to reach the sofa.

Photographs by Karen Shell

"I believe in timeless designs, but I also appreciate a little bit of trend, a touch of the unexpected. Trendy elements are best incorporated as accents that can be updated without disrupting the integrity of the interior design."

—Judy Fox

ABOVE: I wanted the dining room window to look bigger, more prominent, so I visually widened it with graciously gathered silk draperies. The shape of the table and chairs echoes the architectural detailing.

FACING PAGE: Whenever possible, I like to make rooms multifunctional. The laundry room easily doubles as a butler's pantry: The square counter-height table works well for folding clothes or staging hors d'oeuvres. The eclectic variety of surfaces and finishes—the painted and glazed cabinetry, granite countertop surrounding the farm sink and the teal-colored piece with the peeling paint finish—gives the room a well-established look. The homeowners' teal cabinet and antique toy collection, cherished possessions, were a bit tricky to incorporate into the residence, but the laundry room is the perfect place for them.
Photographs by Karen Shell

"Even the most beautiful spaces still need to be functional, or they won't be fully enjoyed."

—Judy Fox

LEFT: I worked with a cabinetmaker to achieve the perfect style, scale and finish of the powder room's mahogany cabinet with custom cloisonné sink. Complementing the fine woodwork, the wall treatment is bold—a high gloss, slightly metallic faux finish.

FACING PAGE: The sunroom is a personal sanctuary, a retreat from the world. I oriented the space toward the wall of windows and lush foliage, careful to select furnishings that created a definite sense of place without distracting from the natural beauty. The softness of the sofa, interesting swirl of the rug and bold stripe of the chairs really produce a wonderful ambience.

Photographs by Karen Shell

STUDIO WETZ ■ RISING...A GALLERY

Dallas, Texas

"Good design should feel
natural in a space and make an
environment more comfortable."

—Bryan Wetz

ABOVE: I designed a contemporary credenza-buffet ideally to be used as a television stand or for storage. To achieve a mid-century look, I conceptualized a modern design, which is seven feet long by 28 inches high. The cabinet's solid wood exterior shell is painted in a high-gloss white finish; the smooth sliding doors are natural rosewood sealed with clear lacquer. I have been designing custom wood furniture since 1997. This prototype piece marks the first in my signature series of this mid-century style.

FACING PAGE: The lounge area is replete with a gentleman's bar and game and dining tables; my custom wood design elements add warmth to the urban space. I designed a traditional-style bar made of solid walnut hardwood and walnut burl—it is clearly the focal point. Refined architectural details, classic columns and well-crafted millwork create a handsome and inviting Old World ambience.
Photographs by Matthew Tilbury

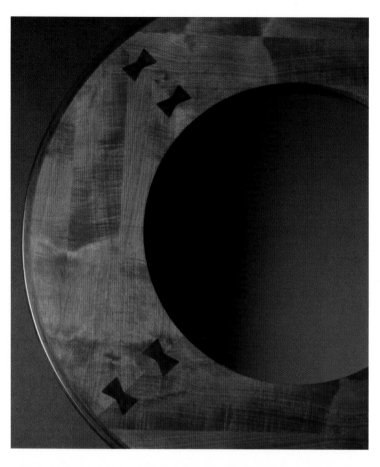

"My design philosophy is about creating furniture with practical style, simplicity and quality craftsmanship."

—Bryan Wetz

RIGHT: I fabricated 55 Marbles, an eye-catching sculptural side table using modern technology and traditional construction techniques. Individual rounds of wood are stacked on center rods with half-inch spacers between layers. Its white high-gloss finish contrasts with a rainbow of shooter marbles encircling the top.

FACING PAGE LEFT: Designed to coordinate with one of my tables, the round mirror frame is made of fiddleback maple and walnut hardwood with classic butterfly joints. Stained a natural teak color, the two-inch-thick, solid pecan wood table is designed to offer ease of use and lasting beauty.

FACING PAGE RIGHT: Intended as a sofa table or entry console combining walnut hardwood and fiddleback maple, the piece is modern with an Asian influence. The imported wood is stained a rich umber tone. I often use eco-friendly, exotic and domestic woods in my furniture designs as they have such interesting characteristics.
Photographs by Matthew Tilbury

"I emphasize functionality in each custom piece. We lose that in our mass production world."

—Bryan Wetz

ABOVE: Built-in cabinetry design takes all forms. One gourmet kitchen design features custom maple millwork. The office of a 1930s Tudor-style home was originally a bedroom, so I designed a white painted and lacquered library shelving unit with a center cabinet that opens into the original closet, seamlessly integrating with the existing architecture. A Texas-style entertainment center of pine and poplar underwent a multiple-step process. We painted it burnt orange, distressed it with chains and nails for an antique effect, painted it cream and sanded parts then stain-washed the surface.

FACING PAGE: I created an office space that is earthy and modern with furniture design made of rift-cut white oak; its minimalist, linear grain makes an impressive conference table. The matching wall cabinetry has a sliding door above a slim granite countertop, so it conveniently opens to the adjacent kitchen becoming a foodservice station.
Photographs by Matthew Tilbury

"I meditate on nature, relating most to its tranquility. I look for gestures in the trees and hand-weld copper and bronze to capture the essence of form."

—Rick Bell-Borja

ABOVE & FACING PAGE: Using traditional hand-welding techniques with bronze and recycled copper as my medium, I create each piece with sensitivity and attention to detail. The fine art of metalwork allows me to make wall sculptures and freestanding pieces for an international clientele. As a second-generation artist, I have been welding sculptures since the early '80s. Nature inspires all that I do. Creating metalwork trees, Monterey cypress and native Saguaro cacti is my forte, but I have also been commissioned to create wildlife sculptures. The 50-inch by 43-inch copper-and-bronze *Steadfast Oak* sculpture evokes strength and beauty from root to branch. I hand-painted each hand-welded leaf with acrylic paint to achieve the most natural colorations, allowing the bronze to show through. My original three-dimensional art pieces can be custom designed for niches and hard-to-fit spaces.
Photographs by Julie Lucas

"I strive to emulate the 'chaotic harmony' of trees; metalworking allows me to portray windswept motion in one harmonious creation."

—Rick Bell-Borja

ABOVE: Aspen trees have eye-catching beauty with their rounded leaves that twist and flutter in the breeze. I created a six-foot-tall aspen grove design to work specifically in a home interior, but any dimensions can be accommodated. Large-scale works are often displayed in public installations—indoors or outdoors—while private homes tend to require smaller pieces. Metal is a versatile medium, and I adapt my designs to suit the space. The quaking aspen of North America is known for its leaves turning spectacular tints of red and yellow early in the autumn season. I hand-painted the textured bronze leaves a deep rust color and the tree bark white for a realistic effect.

Photographs courtesy of Bell-Borja Studios

FACING PAGE: My *Windswept Mighty Oak* sculpture reflects motion much like an asymmetrical cypress tree. Each wall sculpture is derived from a freehand drawing to become an original work of art. Leaves are made of hand-welded bronze; I hand-painted the metal foliage in multicolored orange hues, but any seasonal color preference can be created. First, I draw the roots on paper; then I hand-weld them from copper, coat them with bronze, layer main branches and attach individual leaves. As a final finish, I apply a clear coating to protect the sculpture so it will last for generations. The creative welding process is time-intensive, and each step requires attention to detail.

Photographs by Julie Lucas

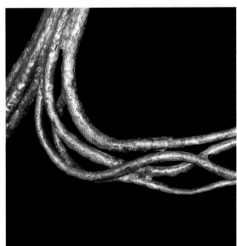

CARL MOORE ANTIQUES

Houston, Texas

"The juxtaposition of antique furnishings with contemporary art creates an exciting envelope for living."

—Geoffrey Westergaard

ABOVE: We acquired reclaimed wrought-iron pieces from France and transformed them into a pair of unique lamps with custom Belgian linen-and-silk shades. Placed atop an English table, the hallway vignette has historic appeal punctuated with vibrant contemporary art. To breathe new life into a space, authentic 19th-century Italian antiques were used differently from their intended function; the original beauty is retained and the room now has uncommon 21st-century flair.

FACING PAGE: Italian Renaissance mirrors and accessories artfully appoint a foyer to create interest and enhance the first impression experience. A French 1930s cast-concrete dolphin garden planter brings the outdoors in for an unexpected interpretation.
Photographs by Carl Moore Antiques

"For a fresh aesthetic, there should be a balanced edge between historical and modern pieces in a space."

—Geoffrey Westergaard

ABOVE: Integrating antiques into contemporary spaces is our forte. Exquisite lamps were made by transforming 18th-century Italian hand-carved walnut putti; we positioned them on the granite bar to create a subtle distinction between the open concept kitchen and dining area. An English mahogany dining table maintains tradition and is complemented by French Louis XV and XVI chairs with caned and upholstered backs to echo the lighter wood tones of the home's cabinetry.

FACING PAGE TOP: A procession through the ages, three periods of antique furniture are commingled beautifully. The traditional living room has a contemporary attitude with exquisite French antiques showcased on a subdued carpet. Vivid orange silk draperies and rich upholstered seating define the au courant ambience. Editing the room using our less is more philosophy creates an air of spaciousness.

FACING PAGE BOTTOM: Specializing in English, Continental and Chinese antiques, our emporium is a trusted resource for imported furnishings and interior design consultation. An exemplary Biedermeier period chair was reupholstered with contemporary textiles to contrast the French walnut side table featuring bronzes from Thailand and Burma. Good interior design strategically places antique furniture amid architecture and fine art to form a relevant style statement; the pieces almost speak to each other.
Photographs by Carl Moore Antiques

'Curtain Couture' Luxury Window-Wear

Dallas, Texas

"European drapery designs inspire layers of timeless elegance. Quality and attention to detail can never be compromised."

—Mary Ann Young

ABOVE: Fine window treatments are an investment. The scalloped detail of the cornice plays "crown" to the flirty under-swags. Both layers have been trimmed to define the treatment. The delicate hand-beaded silk jacquard is an exclusive textile embellished with copper and brass embroidery. This is one example of the many exquisite limited production imports that we source from Europe and Asia.

FACING PAGE: Documented in 1890, the historic French design in the Louis XIV style was chosen for its tailored but soft romantic elegance, perfect for a luxurious master suite. We have a collection of more than 400 historic European designs dating back to the 18th and 19th centuries. Re-creating historic treatments is a labor of love; patterns no longer exist. Our highly skilled pattern-makers must properly scale each design and draft a pattern before our expert seamstress can create a "proof" in muslin for adjustments and final approval. Only then is the fabric cut.
Photographs by Danny Piassick

"Whether contemporary or traditional, the room is not complete until the windows are properly dressed."

—Mary Ann Young

LEFT: The dramatic 20-foot vaulted ceiling left the formal living room lacking intimacy. The design we chose provides elegant layers including a hand-gilded wood cornice that tops a tapestry-upholstered lambrequin spanning 15 feet with silk taffeta drapery framing the treed views. We drew inspiration from a French portiere design dating back to the early 1800s. Portiere dressings and drapery originated as a necessity to cover drafty halls and doorways. The more elaborate designs with extensive wood mouldings were seen only in the most affluent homes.

FACING PAGE TOP: Chosen for its masculine and formal style, the historic German pelmet design from the 1800s features a bold medallion fabric with jet black silk trim punctuating the intricate hemline. Topping the pelmet is an ornate gilded wood cornice. Our custom millwork cornices are artfully combined, built and hand-finished to design specifications by our highly skilled artisans. Designed to dress a pair of corner windows and frame the wooded views, the treatment completes the Dallas dream home's library.

FACING PAGE BOTTOM: Wide banks of windows are difficult to dress when traditional swags are too fussy. Creating visual interest over an 18-foot span requires careful orchestration of details. In a traditional Southern home, two layers of scalloped valance were designed with knife pleat clusters. The green silk under-valance, peeking out from behind, is included solely for the definition of the hemline's curvature. Additionally, two layers of drapery add interest and function. The outer layer provides continuity with the top treatment, and an under layer of striped silk taffeta echoes the fresh colors of this sophisticated home.

Photographs by Danny Piassick

DWIGHT BENNETT

Phoenix, Arizona

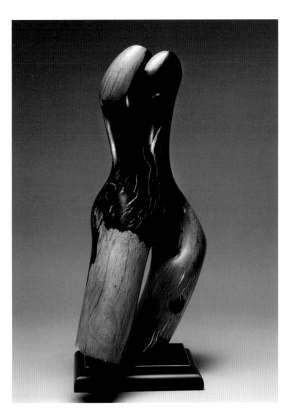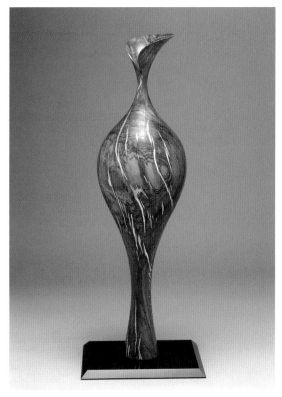

"My reason for being is wood sculpture—to create wonderful shapes that move and have a voice of color and scream so loud that everyone will hear."

—Dwight Bennett

ABOVE: I hand-carved *Dancing with Silver* out of natural ironwood, a tree that exclusively grows in the Arizona desert, twice the hardness of marble. Using carving chisels to create its shape, grinding and finally hand-sanding to smooth my design, I reinterpreted the wood into a figurative form symbolic of the female body. Pure silver veins run through the piece. *Whispering Willow* is an olive wood vessel hollowed out to accentuate the feel. Its contemporary shape is reminiscent of female form with its flowing movement; the wood vessel is inlaid with silver castings for added grace and harmony. My sculptures are mounted on black quartz for private display and for exhibitions across the United States.

FACING PAGE: Olive wood from Israel was the medium for my hand-carved sculpture entitled *Fantasia*, inspired by the explosion of sea waves in Walt Disney's animated classic. I sculpted the piece, drew where I wanted precious metal inlaid and sent it to the foundry for castings based on my specifications. A mold was formed to make the pure silver inlays; I cemented them into the pre-carved crevices, ground them back down to the surface of the wood and hand-oiled the sculpture for a fine finish. My signature silver inlays create contrast against the natural wood with gleaming highlights. I take things that are still and make them move through wood sculpting.

Photographs courtesy of Dwight Bennett and Rose

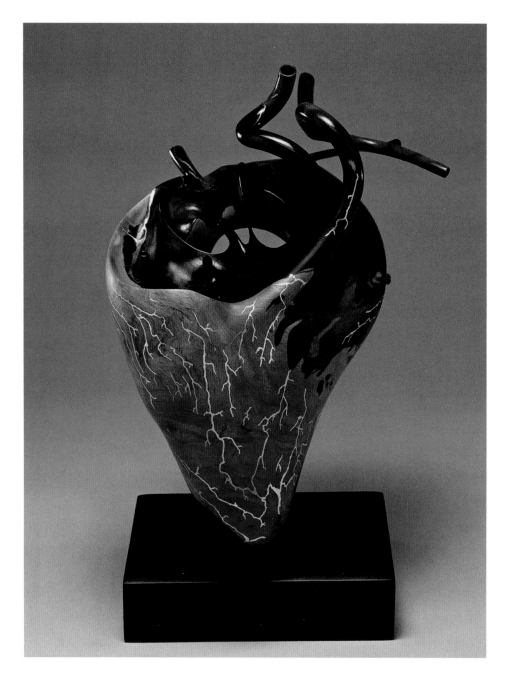

"Wood speaks to me. I give it a voice that has never been heard before. Then, I enhance each sculpture with pure silver striations for flow and harmony."

—Dwight Bennett

RIGHT: I chose ironwood for my hand-carved *Venus* sculpture; intended as a public installation, it now resides in a private collection. The 500-pound, 15-foot-high sculpture preserved a desert tree—ironwoods often live for up to 500 years—for eternity. With subtle silver highlights to enhance the abstract curves, the piece pays homage to the power and beauty of female form. I used pulleys to hoist the three-ton trunk at my studio in preparation for carving with an axe, a power saw, chisels and mallets. As a "take away" artist, I remove wood to give birth to my vision just as Michelangelo chiseled marble away to reveal the form within.

FACING PAGE TOP: As a wood sculptor I work in two realms: Mother Nature and figurative form. I hand-carved *Life* in 1972 as my interpretation of the human heart, made from ironwood for enduring beauty. People can almost touch the life experience with its dark vein-like structures. This museum piece stands 14 inches tall and has numerous cast-silver veins. I used ultra-fine sandpaper to create its smooth finish then hand-oiled the wood to bring out its color with a satin sheen.

FACING PAGE BOTTOM: *Pink Bougainvillea* is a 28-inch vessel that I hand-carved from rare, centuries-old African pink ivory wood, a sacred wood of Zulu chiefs. Its exotic color inspired my design. My work is a poem and a statement; I never use synthetic stains to enhance or alter the wood because it is unnatural. Wood's honesty and true colors must be revealed. I created pure silver lines to move through the piece from the delicate top to the bottom, as if pouring clear water over the wood.

Photographs by Dwight Bennett and Rose

JOHN GREGORY STUDIO ▪ ELIAS GUERRERO LIGHTING

Dallas, Texas

"The beauty of perfectly restored antique chandeliers, with their dazzling crystals and hand-blown glass, has a transformative power."

—Elias Guerrero

ABOVE: A late 18th-century garden lantern made of artistically cast iron features scrollwork and the traditional acanthus leaf design. We discovered the imported hand-crafted piece in France, probably from a château estate. Its painted green color is authentic and subtly timeworn, but we rewired the antique lamp into a grand hallway fixture that softly glows with discreet, low-voltage halogen lighting.

FACING PAGE: I restored a pair of late 19th-century Versailles chandeliers, painstakingly repairing broken crystal pieces using transparent ultraviolet glue and reforming bent metal frames. The dramatic 10-foot-tall lighting fixture boasts scalloped lead crystal prisms and pendants. Both chandeliers were electrified with sockets and faux candles, as they were originally designed to hold beeswax candles for illumination in palaces or homes of nobility. The chandeliers now grace a luxurious dressing room.
Photographs courtesy of John Gregory Studio

"Exquisite lighting creates ambience. Finding the right period piece sets the tone, becoming jewelry for the home."

—John Gregory

ABOVE LEFT: Ornately cast ormolu forms with long curved arms are characteristic of late 18th-century French chandeliers. We carefully restored the Gothic-inspired iron fixture with carved and gilded wood to recapture its historic luster. The intricate piece was rebuilt: Broken wood elements were replaced, hand-carved and regilded with pure 22-karat gold leaf, and new faux candles were added and electrified to meet current lighting standards.

ABOVE RIGHT: The art of Venetian glassmaking is revered the world over. A pale aubergine color, the 1930s hand-blown Murano glass pendant provides a warm ambience and flowing aesthetic. Its bronze metal framework showcases a neoclassic shell motif. We completely rewired the timeless Art Deco period piece to create ideal ambient lighting.

FACING PAGE: Our elite sources in Europe present us with rare antique lighting pieces destined to be restored. We imported a pair of impressive, 12-foot-high, 19th-century chandeliers with detailed bronze filigree tiers still intact; the fine metalwork inspired our remodeled design. We hand strung custom-stamped bronze medallions for a unique suspended effect. The chandeliers originally glowed by candlelight, but we electrified them for modern-day use.
Photographs courtesy of John Gregory Studio

"I love the organic nature of stone—no two pieces look, feel, smell, carve or finish out exactly the same. To choose the perfect block, I take into account the desired aesthetic as well as where and how the sculpture will be displayed."

—Davis Cornell

ABOVE: Carved from Indiana limestone, *Pigeonholed* is 78 inches tall, 38 wide and 10 deep. I used a drill, a hammer and a chisel for the square niches and the circle that pierces the full depth of the stone; I finished it with a bush chisel and files. The piece's title is sort of a funny story. While I was sculpting, the design made me think of the pigeonhole wall system where I'd check the mail for my high school Latin teacher. I researched various meanings of "pigeonhole" and really connected with the irony of the concept: to lay aside with the intention of ignoring or forgetting.
Photograph by Phil Hollenbeck

FACING PAGE: When a couple commissioned me to sculpt buffet tables—to function as room dividers—for their San Angelo home, the only direction they gave was "mesquite trees," so I basically gleaned my inspiration from a stick of firewood. The buffet tables look like wood, but they are actually Cordova cream limestone—I stained the stone to accentuate the deepest areas and make the bases look like genuine tree trunks. I freeform carved each of the legs and then sketched out the bas-relief of the tabletops.
Photograph by Gary Blockley

LEFT: I sculpted the limestone entry table from a photograph of crepe myrtle limbs lashed to a glass tabletop—my clients saw the idea in an antique shop and wanted a contemporary interpretation of the motif. The project was extremely site-specific, so I designed the piece to make the most of the accent wall's constraints: I curved the tabletop edge toward the kitchen wall so the door wouldn't swing into it. Because the piece would be enjoyed from three sides, I made it almost three dimensional with fully rounded limbs going several layers deep. And to counterbalance the brightness of the extant canister lights as well as create a nighttime focal point, I installed LEDs beneath the tabletop.

FACING PAGE TOP: Before studying in Pietrasanta, Italy, and interning with a stone carver in Dallas, my medium of choice was laminated plywood. I designed the screens consecutively as functional art; they started out as a simple means to conceal and then proved themselves as pieces of art. The plywood is turned on the profile edge to expose the layers. I experimented with the illusion of bending the thin strips of wood, creating depth and an interesting geometry.

FACING PAGE BOTTOM LEFT: While the bird of paradise relief is set into an exterior brick wall, it was very much created for enjoyment from within the home. Flanking the window that it's enjoyed from are two paintings of tropical birds. I was commissioned to complement the homeowners' paintings, and I took a liberal stylistic approach in order to maximize the impact of the medium.

FACING PAGE BOTTOM RIGHT: I sculpted the three-foot-square freestanding panel as a gift from board members of the San Angelo Health Foundation to the retiring chairman, who was instrumental in making the foundation's new headquarters possible. While the building construction was still underway, I began the project: I reviewed the architectural drawings, visited the site with a photographer friend and decided on a majestic perspective of the building from across the water. Originally, I'd hoped to sculpt from the actual building material, but it wasn't quite up to art grade, so I went with antique Lueders limestone for its rich tonal qualities and ability to hold small details. I was invited to help present the piece to the former chairman as well as explain its composition and my methodology, which is always a privilege for an artist.

Photographs by Gary Blockley

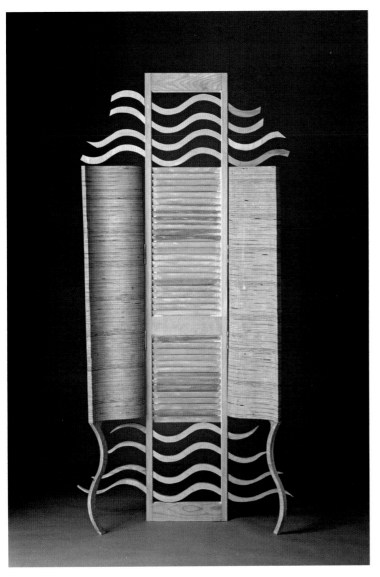

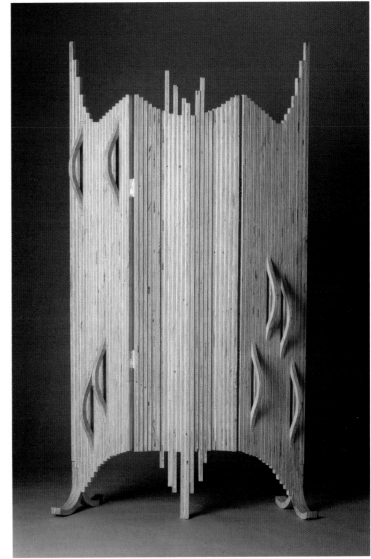

LE LOUVRE FRENCH ANTIQUES

Dallas, Texas

"Before I acquire a piece, it must speak to me. Then, and only then, can it be in my antiques showroom for others to love."

—Annick McNally

ABOVE: The rare finds we discover for our discerning clientele include unique 18th- and 19th-century pieces shipped directly to our design district showroom after each shopping excursion to France. The majestic bibliothèque is from a boiserie room or classic wood-paneled room. Tapestry chairs, the Louis XV-style chest of drawers and the Boulle-style writing desk with inlaid leather are a few of the exquisite pieces we have found. Designer accessories include circa 1860 bronze dore candelabras on marble bases, a bronze cartel and a signed French bronze statue.

FACING PAGE: Our traditional French château vignette boasts an exquisite 18th-century Verdure tapestry suspended behind a rare, hand-carved Louis XV-style chest of drawers with bronze hardware. A regal pair of gilt-metal 19th-century urns from a convent have cobalt blue enameled insets and hold gilt-metal jonquil bouquets.
Photographs by Danny Piassick

"We attract designers and architects from around the world who desire period furniture and antique architecturals including stone mantels, doors and fountains. Antiques possess the beauty of their rich heritage, which instantly creates authentic ambience."

—Annick McNally

ABOVE LEFT: A Francophile's dream, the walnut Chaise en Bateau is period Régence from the early 1700s and features hand-carved floral and foliate details. The piece simply awaits upholstered cushions.

ABOVE RIGHT: Weathered with age, the early 18th-century painted Italian entry door can be also used as a dramatic headboard; the reproduction French door was made in Provence with authentic detailing and pewter hardware. Americans seek fine French antiques to suit their everyday lifestyles. For example, a wonderful French chest of drawers can become a magnificent powder room vanity.

FACING PAGE: Specializing in antique French furnishings, accessories and architecturals, we cater to designers with a flair for the unusual. Our showroom boasts a Louis XVI-style giltwood console, Louis XIII tapestry chairs, a carved walnut desk, bronze dore chenets and a pair of small Louis XV-style toile bedroom chairs—only a few of the found treasures on display.

Photographs by Danny Piassick

PAN AMERICAN ART PROJECTS

"Fine art produced by today's artists is often a response to and manifestation of what is happening in our society. Viewers can discover the artist's message or build on it through their own personal experiences."

—Cris Worley

ABOVE: Pan American Art Projects first opened its doors in 2003 and later relocated to a new light-filled space located amid the world-class Dallas Design District. Our gallery specializes in art of North and South America with the mission to connect cultures by presenting and exhibiting premier artists from very different regions concurrently. The Dallas and Miami galleries showcase emerging and established artists as well as secondary market work of note, offering collectors profound aesthetic beauty, exquisite craftsmanship and thought-provoking subject matter.

FACING PAGE: Cuban artist Gustavo Acosta's acrylic-on-canvas entitled *Destiny* is an impressive piece by its massive size alone. The artist's dramatic depiction of a partially submerged ship in a stormy sea brings to mind the end of a dream, where the destination is never reached. Acosta's daring use of vibrant color and skillful technique draws one into the image of doom.

Photographs by Pan American Art Projects

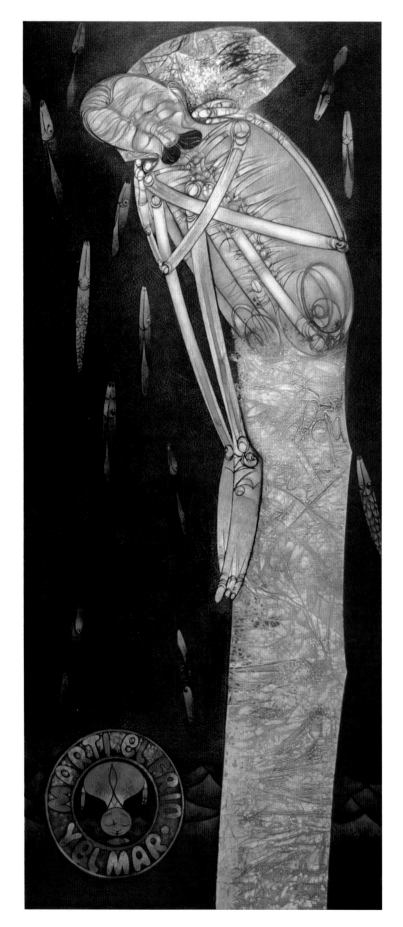

"Acquiring a piece of fine art enriches our lives immeasurably."

—Cris Worley

TOP: Dallas artist-sculptor Rusty Scruby applies his mathematical and musical mind through mixed-media reconstruction. First taking photographs and printing in multiples, he cuts out the images and weaves them together to create three-dimensional forms on canvas. Textural with facets of interlocking hexagonal shapes, the photos become a secondary aspect and the art becomes more about the construction itself. Scruby's aptly named *Cello* has a bold tree image resembling the curved neck of the classical instrument.

BOTTOM: Ted Larsen works in Santa Fe using recycled metal as his medium. Environmentally conscious, he reiterates the importance of being green through artful expressions. Larsen cuts shapes, arranges them in composition and adheres the metal to substrate material. One can appreciate the beauty of intrinsic metal colors in his mosaic-like assemblages. Sometimes the artist distresses pieces to add a rough-hewn quality yet the effect is precise and contemporary.

FACING PAGE LEFT: Gallery artist Pedro Pablo Oliva is a renowned Cuban painter whose work represents a passionate vision to underscore his homeland's political history and social climate through themed artistic expression. Oliva's poignant oil painting depicts hero José Marti, an honored poet, patriot and martyr of Cuban Independence. The artist is known for elongated, exaggerated or morphed figures; his detailed image becomes a political commentary that engages the viewer with its surreal style.

FACING PAGE TOP: From El Salvador, Ronald Morán experienced times of war, and his creative themes raise awareness of violence, both large-scale and domestic. The artist takes common objects and wraps them in cottony fibers to soften the edges, blurring the line between utilitarian function and their potential as weapons. The five-foot-tall oil painting mimics a photograph with light and shadow, deftly formed by brushstrokes of black and white pigment.

FACING PAGE BOTTOM: Graphite on canvas is the preferred medium of Cuban artist Lopez Pardo. His powerful use of graphite sticks—a minimalist approach to composition combined with strong realist drawing techniques—impacts the viewer. He contrasts negative space with extraordinary images that often include crude shacks and ominous tornadoes. In a monochromatic piece, the artist communicates our human vulnerability by juxtaposing a fragile, manmade structure with clouds symbolizing the intensity of nature.

Photographs by Pan American Art Projects

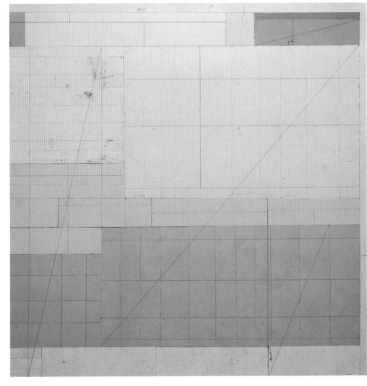

PAT MONROE ANTIQUES

Austin, Texas — Dallas, Texas

"Antiques connect us to history and many world cultures. Create an ambience of timeless beauty by collecting authentic pieces."

—Pat Monroe

ABOVE: We established the room's focal point with a French 1840s solid walnut dining table. I love the beautiful, natural patina of aged wood. The impressive dark walnut buffet with classically French carved drawers and doors is a grand example of the period. I am drawn to artistic antique pieces that also serve a useful purpose for today's lifestyles.

FACING PAGE: We discover rare finds when we travel abroad. Our shop specializes in importing fine French and European antiques from the 17th, 18th and 19th centuries. Recently, I fell in love with 19th-century Swedish furniture with its traditional milk paint finish. It is perfect for creating a casual refinement as depicted in this vignette. We combined the light, white Swedish pieces with gold framed paintings and maps, a gray French mirror, a pastel rug and dramatic candle sconces.
Photographs by Pat Monroe

"Surround yourself with antiques you love so you'll relive that feeling each time you enter the room."

—Pat Monroe

ABOVE: We transformed an antique Parisian ironwork balcony into a custom console table by adding a zinc top. The pair of 19th-century French bergères makes wonderful formal seating. A black and gold chinoiserie tray-table and small commode, circa 1700s from Paris, were great finds from one of our European shopping trips. Imported French and Italian chandeliers sparkle with exquisite crystal and enliven any room. We believe that antiques and art should go hand-in-hand. Our perfectly picked collection of oil paintings by European artists from the 18th and 19th centuries can either complement traditional rooms or add unexpected contrast to contemporary décor.

FACING PAGE: Interior design ideas often begin with one fabulous historical piece. An impressive 19th-century signed tapestry depicts the lovely Empress Eugénie, wife of Napoleon III, with her ladies-in-waiting. The delicate hand-painted design on our country French tall clock is enhanced by the rich carving and lines of the dining table, chairs and buffet. We recommend blending the luxurious with the relaxed, as we did by creating the French daybed made from antique headboards and runners, reupholstered in a luscious pale blue silk, mixed with fringed, tasseled pillows and shadowy tone-on-tone toile pillows. Adorning the walls is an 18th-century Trumeau mirror with its romantic angel motif and gilded sunburst mirrors.
Photographs by Pat Monroe

"What is this obsession with antiquity? A good old rug was once a good new rug. Look for quality, condition and artistic merit in rugs of any age."

—Mehdi Abedi, Ph.D.

ABOVE & FACING PAGE: As educators and experts on hand-woven rugs, we have earned a reputation as a knowledgeable resource for homeowners, interior designers and connoisseurs. We believe in sharing our passion for this ancient yet dynamic art form, which has beautified palaces, cottages and tents for more than 3,000 years. Most Persian rugs are named after cities, villages and tribes from which they originate; weavers use wool, silk and cotton to express regional symbolism through pattern and color. Highly collectible rugs have withstood the test of time, surviving to teach us of the peoples, places and cultures behind them. Antique or new, our rugs are works of art from Iran, Turkey, India and other countries where textile design and hand-weaving remain vital components of culture. Vase Design rug by HJR.
Photographs by Don A. Hoffman

"The rug is an anchor piece of a room. It is a personal and meaningful expression of purpose and style from which an interior design organically unfolds."

—Lisa Slappey, Ph.D.

ABOVE & FACING PAGE: It is a myth that the best rugs are necessarily those with the most knots per square inch. Evaluate the rug's overall quality and condition, paying special attention to the harmony and artistic merit rendered through fine materials, good design and skilled workmanship. Like a masterful work of art, a hand-woven rug becomes an enduring element and, with proper care, an heirloom for future generations to enjoy. Hand-woven rugs should be washed and repaired by reputable specialists to retain their value, beauty and luster. As fundamental components of design, rugs integrate the values of East and West, contemporary and traditional, old and new, simplicity and complexity. Elegant and magical, a unique rug can transform any room.
Photographs by Don A. Hoffman

"Authentic rustic furniture, art and accessories of original design, made by talented craftsmen and artisans, bring an abode to life with quality and unique style."

—Natividad Rios

ABOVE & FACING PAGE: Whether a sprawling country ranch, hacienda or rustic Southwest residence, we work to further define the homeowner's desire for original furnishings, executing each piece with exquisite detail. We have talented, experienced craftsmen who possess a true passion for producing uniquely beautiful, hand-carved pieces for interior and exterior spaces. Using leather, hand-forged iron, mesquite, mango, pine and other exotic woods, our traditional designs create an atmosphere of warmth, age and authenticity. Specializing in custom furniture and décor, we often collaborate with residential architects and interior design professionals to comply with specifications. Our luxurious collection of fine furnishings, exceptional art and accessories—handmade in the spirit of the Southwest with Old World textures and colors—gives distinctive style and character to any dwelling.

Photographs courtesy of Rios Interiors

AJ's Landscaping & Design, page 287

Berghoff Design Group, page 275

living the elements

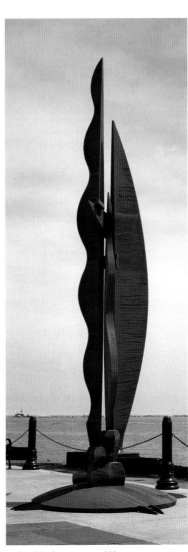

A roll-up-his-sleeves kind of man, Jeff Berghoff is an entrepreneur with roots in the design-build business. Working with craftsmen to create three-dimensional spaces, he engages architects and artisans with the goal of achieving the ultimate aesthetic. Jeff studied both landscape architecture and horticulture at Arizona State University, so it was only natural that he founded his own residential boutique design firm specializing in luxury landscaping and construction management in 1997.

With a passion for design, Jeff creates some of Scottsdale's most talked about landscapes and showcase gardens for elite clientele. Jeff collaborates with award-winning architects and custom builders, working on numerous projects that require his knowledge of the desert terrain. His team of professionals has in-depth experience working in the region and a certified horticulturist is on staff to select appropriate plantings. The firm is acclaimed for having designed traditional formal gardens and spectacular outdoor environments that seamlessly integrate with new or established residences. Jeff is renowned for creating remarkable manmade landscapes and hardscapes on private properties throughout Arizona. Experts in designing flowering gardens, manicured lawns, stone walkways, fountains, palm-lined courtyards, dream pools and patios for entertaining, Berghoff Design Group creates luxurious landscapes with enduring beauty.

"When done right, landscape design can create sensory moments in time and space."

—Jeff Berghoff

BERGHOFF DESIGN GROUP

"Inspiration stems from desire, but dreams become reality through a detailed aesthetic vision."

—Jeff Berghoff

RIGHT: We designed the summer garden for a woman who wanted varied species of flowers ideal for cutting and arranging. Guests are drawn in by the colorful bouquet, artfully planted to grace the entrance of an Old Hollywood-style home with its simple, classic lines. The architecture is a sublime backdrop for the tousled, organic mélange of rose bushes, lavender, clipped myrtle hedges, pansies and alyssum. We added a desert ironwood tree as the focal point; its branches and leaves cast shadows on the home's façade, creating a mesmerizing show when the wind blows.

PREVIOUS PAGES: As part of a remodel project, we designed a sleek, contemporary pool and spa environment that flows as one space from interior to exterior for an iconic mid-century home on Camelback Mountain. The infinity-edge pool has water spills on three sides and a patio, spa and firepit area extending out on the same plane as the home. Our glass railing design allows for clear Arizona sunset views; a mesquite tree contrasts the crisp, sharp lines of the home.

Photographs by Bill Timmerman

"An outdoor setting must be an extension of the residence's architectural character."

—Jeff Berghoff

ABOVE: The elegant Tuscan façade of a new home inspired us to create a formal classical garden with cypress and olive trees, rose bushes, gated secret gardens and an inner courtyard with fountains. The architects designed the two-and-a-half-acre estate to look like an established Italian villa. We used pea gravel for walkways and imported stone to project a sense of permanence and European antiquity.
Photograph by Bill Timmerman

FACING PAGE: Our goal was to exude the character of the home in keeping with its original classic style. Majestic Canary Island date palms line the front yard of the historic 1920s home. We designed and reorganized the front yard to form a strong axial alignment to the street: A manicured grass lawn with rectangular stepping stones leads to the enchanting stone fountain with a glimpse of the bluestone patio beyond. Choice materials were used to create a special place to entertain alfresco while potted annuals and flowerbeds accent the environment.
Photograph by Wes Johnson

"A home and garden should be married to reflect one seamless union."

—Jeff Berghoff

ABOVE & FACING PAGE: We created a timeless swimming pool to fit with the classic 1920s residence and centered it in the middle of the lawn for soft, natural grass underfoot. Formalized classical hedges surround the pool for privacy. The lap pool has a concealed diving platform and multiple spill fountains for a soothing effect. We remodeled a backyard garden to give residents an experience reminiscent of places they visited in the South of France. Rustic limestone steps and hand-laid stone courtyards blend with a myriad of potted flowers, fragrant herbs and a grass-encircled water feature for a quaint Provence ambience.

Photographs by Wes Johnson

"We strive to create outdoor environments that exude the personality of the residents."

—Jeff Berghoff

ABOVE: In charming European style, we designed a front courtyard filled with flowering beds of annual plantings that generously spill over the walkway for a lush invitation to the home. A tranquil mood greets guests with the central antique birdbath, formal privacy walls and authentic inlaid entrance tiles. We artfully created an easy-to-manage environment that exudes a true Tuscan atmosphere based on the homeowner's dream. We believe that professional landscaping is a holistic process. It should envelop creative design, construction, lighting and ease of care for both residential and commercial projects.
Photograph by Bill Timmerman

FACING PAGE: The desert provides challenges for landscape design, but with thoughtful planning and construction management the indoor-outdoor connection can be achieved. For an Old Hollywood-style home with three tiers of terraces, we designed a classic "lifestyle garden" on the back veranda to take in the spectacular sight of Camelback Mountain. We master planned tennis courts and a green lawn area to fit the grounds. Our team used tumbled brick on the patio for an earthy, cobblestone effect while the circular fire pit with its orange glow makes a warm conversation area.
Photograph by CAPS

"When home gardens are well-designed, they are surprisingly simple to maintain."

—Jeff Berghoff

RIGHT: Our certified horticulturist knows what will thrive in the region, whether aquatic plants, flowers, shrubs or trees. We transformed a rustic water trough into a quiet koi pond with water reeds and iris amid natural rocks for an unexpected Zen retreat. To remodel the adobe home's swimming pool, we framed the classic shape with soft grass, thus eliminating a hard-surface deck. We lined the pool with mother-of-pearl tiles for shimmer and trimmed it with new coping. Year-round annual gardens that are always in bloom give a welcome burst of color.
Photographs by Bill Timmerman

FACING PAGE: We designed the backyard landscape for casa azul—a quintessential Santa Barbara-style home—with its winding staircase leading to the rear loggia. Our vision was to create an intimate courtyard effect with grassy areas; we installed an impressive blue and white hand painted Mexican tile fountain as the yard's centerpiece in keeping with the home's architectural genre.
Photograph by Wes Johnson

"The landscape should be a seamless extension of a home's architecture."

—A.J. Benys

Painting "live" landscapes and creating breathtaking outdoor spaces is the specialty of designer A.J. Benys, award-winning horticulturist-artist. The hybrid designer studied horticulture at Sam Houston State University and went on to earn his second degree in landscape architecture from Texas A&M; this cross-pollination has proven to be an amazing formula for success. Even as a young boy A.J. displayed an artistic gift and love of nature. He created drawings, watercolors and oil paintings of trees and plants, an early indicator of his future passion and profession.

After one college semester abroad, A.J.'s life was forever changed. The European experience with rich cultural roots and centuries-old history was fascinating. The high aesthetic of Italian and French art and architecture, the countryside and formal gardens captured him in a way that would later influence his own designs. In 1982 A.J. founded his namesake residential landscaping and design-build studio, beginning his journey to creating some of Houston's most beautiful private gardens with stunning hardscapes including garden rooms, courtyards and fountains, natural stone patios and swimming pools. Today, A.J.'s consulting team is comprised of credentialed landscape architects and designers, a seasoned installation crew and dedicated staff who consistently demonstrate passion and creativity.

AJ's Landscaping & Design

"Creative challenges inspire our design-build approach."

—A.J. Benys

RIGHT: The narrow backyard presented certain limitations, but we were able to design and build a raised terrace with heated spa and swimming pool using creative brickwork for sculptural definition. An outdoor kitchen with grill and sink is hidden by traditional antique brick. The dry-set flagstone patio was outlined with drought-tolerant zoysia grass while curvilinear planter beds and trellised fencing soften hard lines to create an inviting retreat.

PREVIOUS PAGES: We designed and built a secluded family entertaining space in keeping with the Mediterranean style of the home. The private swimming pool features a shallow sundeck with bubbling fountains. A shaded lounge area and adjacent stucco cabana are accented by native sago palms, Texas mountain laurel and Italian cypress to extend the Tuscan villa feeling; plantings were chosen for a low-maintenance environment. Quality Chino Valley flagstone forms the durable patio of this chic oasis.

Photographs by Blair Michener

"Classical elements and architectural details create an outdoor ambience of elegance."

—A.J. Benys

ABOVE & FACING PAGE: A French-inspired fountain grotto creates architectural interest in the hardscape with a hint of formality that also buffers inner city noise. We created a spillway with relaxing water sounds to drown out unpleasant street clamor. Smooth stucco and cream-colored limestone round out the look with custom hand-carved urns and pedestal planters for vibrant annuals. The raised wall is a hand-laid backdrop of fossilized travertine. Our team designed and built the classic swimming pool veneered in Italian glass tiles for a mosaic effect replete with its bubbling, submerged sundeck.
Photographs by Blair Michener

"An intimate backyard environment feels like a true extension of the home."

—A.J. Benys

ABOVE & FACING PAGE: Mature oaks shade the winding pathway that leads to an outdoor kitchen set further into the yard. We flanked the flagstone walk with kettle-style fire bowls on hand-laid stone pedestals for a dramatic nighttime atmosphere. Our team is ultra sensitive to existing plant life when adding to an established landscape, and we work to preserve nature's beauty wherever possible. We built a cabana house and cocktail pool situated just steps from the back door of the home for convenient access. Natural stone areas and the walkway are edged with dwarf mondo grass to mesh with existing trees. Hardscape elements are important to the overall design of the courtyard space, but we softened the effect with western white clematis vines to create a lush urban retreat.
Photographs by Blair Michener

"An imaginative front yard is like a welcoming work of art."

—A.J. Benys

ABOVE LEFT & RIGHT: Inspired by a formal French château with cast stone and limestone architectural details, we echoed the home's ambience in our manicured landscape and traditional hardscape concept. The side yard's tiered, antique iron fountain was bought at auction and we designed the base around the rare find. To prevent obstruction of the home's front façade, we chose small-scale plantings that will remain less than three feet tall. Smooth bull-nose concrete steps, an acid-washed concrete walkway and balustrade elements combine to create a refined invitation to the gracious home.

FACING PAGE: Enhancing a residence's architecture and drawing people to the main entry is our aim in designing a front yard. The contemporary design for a Mediterranean home had to consider a circular driveway. We wanted it to be decorative yet feel open and eclectic to allow for guest traffic. In the island bed, a bench sits beside the raised planter and pedestal bowl filled with colorful annuals and perennials. The unique checkerboard courtyard is a juxtaposition of hand-cut Milford green flagstone with neatly trimmed zoysia grass squares.
Photographs by Blair Michener

"Lounging areas should draw people out into the yard and invite them to linger."

—A.J. Benys

LEFT & FACING PAGE: Tight backyard patio spaces can be challenging to design. We recommend decorative fences and distinctive lounge furniture, cedar arbors, precast columns and custom elements such as antique brick or open ironwork to give a highly personalized look. Creating a special place for rest and relaxation in the backyard allows residents to enjoy the serenity of nature as an extension of their home with absolute privacy. Even artistically inlaid stone can be outlined with perennial ornamental grass for a luxurious, nature-inspired effect. Climbing vines and potted tropical foliage also bring soothing greenery into focus.

Photographs by Blair Michener

ACCLAIM POOLS

The Woodlands, Texas

"A custom pool should emulate a home's natural setting or mirror its architectural style."

—Steven Toth

ABOVE: Our private pool design for a Mediterranean-style home on forested property required ingenuity. We built the neoclassic pool in a side yard to preserve the shade tree environment; its symmetrical design complements the traditional residence. In keeping with the serene surroundings, decorative geysers provide an audible ambience and an arched cedarwood arbor softens the effect. The retreat features a heated spa situated 60 feet away from the swimming pool, just steps from the master bedroom.

FACING PAGE: We drew terraced design plans to reflect the lakeside home's inspirational setting: A dramatic vanishing-edge pool melds seamlessly into the vista while the gentle spillover enhances the aesthetic with tranquil water sounds. The pool was skillfully built on a slope of non-virgin soil where structural support was critical. The saltwater pool provides a silky swim experience and easy care with ozone sanitization for crystal-clear water. We are highly conscious of the environment; our energy-efficient pools utilize the latest systems with a green emphasis.
Photographs by Laura Caron Photography

"Form, function, safety and sensitivity to the environment are key elements of an artfully designed swimming pool."

—Steven Toth

ABOVE & FACING PAGE: A well-designed pool is a work of art. Whether re-constructions or new creations, timeless swimming pools are best achieved through a blend of good design principles, sound engineering, smart technology and the finest materials. Custom waterscape styles such as natural lagoons, contemporary freeform and classic geometrics each lend a different mood to the outdoor environment. As a Genesis 3 Design Group member our company is held to superior standards, so thoughtful planning and construction are of utmost importance. Exquisite finishes range from glamorous Italian porcelains to colorful emerald-bay pebbled surfaces. We lay premier-quality poolside decks made of natural flagstone, hand-cut stones and honed Turkish travertine pavers. Stately columns, raised rear walls, unique fountains and architectural elements enhance the experience and promise lasting enjoyment.
Photographs by Laura Caron Photography

"Beyond using authentic materials and Old World craftsmanship, we're all about creating a lifestyle for homeowners."

—Patrick Heyl

ABOVE & FACING PAGE: The traditional home has a Spanish Colonial influence, characteristic of those seen throughout beautiful Santa Barbara. We collaborated with the designers and team of craftsmen prior to selecting natural stone from indigenous quarries; our hand-picked stone of varied organic colors, shapes and sizes creates an artistic exterior façade and outdoor extension of the home. For a beachside feeling we designed a negative-edge pool to wrap around the covered porch structure. We engineered and constructed the charming detached pool house replete with a high-tech media room.

Photographs by Coles Hairston Photography

"New home interpretations should possess a classic and timeless quality, paying homage to architectural style origins."

—Patrick Heyl

ABOVE & FACING PAGE: Whether we are commissioned to build a French Country home or an Italian-inspired residential design, we strive to replicate the true genre and era. For example, blasted rubble stone was hand-chiseled and rounded to create a historically accurate effect. Exterior façades, courtyards and poolside loggias reflect the architectural style in every detail, from classic columns to enchanting turrets and enduring clay tile roofing. We construct exclusive homes using Old World techniques executed by local artisans and expert craftsmen who understand that meticulous workmanship equates to a luxurious dwelling.

Photographs by Coles Hairston Photography

MICHAEL ANDERSON

Scottsdale, Arizona

"Through steel sculpture, I unite the strength of tradition, clarity of vision and the spirit of progress, bringing the past into the future."

—Michael Anderson

ABOVE: River rocks, chains and a flat steel bar are insignificant on their own. Are we not like those seemingly insignificant elements—touched by God and transformed from the mundane to the sublime?

FACING PAGE: One work from my Monument Series—fabricated of Cor-Ten steel—is a public installation entitled *Tribal Figment*. The 19-foot sculpture was inspired by majestic rock formations that I viewed from an aerial perspective. Symbolic of a personal milestone, my pieces often mark a turning point of life, remembrances of the past and my step in a new direction. I created the monumental piece by welding hollow steel forms together. The sandblasted finish exposes bare metal to allow even oxidation to occur, giving the sculpture its bright red hue. Rainwater streaked the finish for an interesting effect. First installed at Navy Pier in Chicago, the piece is permanently on public display in Las Vegas.
Photographs by Scott Youmans

"Ornament has to do with visual beauty of a thing—no penetrating depth of character or feeling, only superficiality, validated solely by its aesthetic."

—Michael Anderson

ABOVE & FACING PAGE: My Ornament Series is purely decorative. I hand forge and fabricate steel using blacksmithing techniques then sandblast and darken pieces by firing them in red hot flames. Some sculptural pieces are rubbed with linseed oil for sheen. These often geometric, three-dimensional ornamental forms represent the way in which many people exist: false perfection, using their beauty to allure. Most people will never know what intelligence, work or creative perceptions reside within—like a soul without a home. I created *Opposing Weights with Sphere*, a suspended eight-foot-long ornament framed by weathered steel, to become the poignant centerpiece of a private sculpture garden.
Photographs by Scott Youmans

"A home should reflect the personality and lifestyle of its owners. If not, it will appear pretentious and be much less inviting to guests."

—Scott Sangalli

ABOVE: We designed a French Country estate reminiscent of a rural château, carefully adhering to requisite elements of scale and proportion. The interior, elevations and outdoor living areas demonstrate the importance of consistency between all architectural elements. Artisans and craftsmen combined meticulous millwork, cast stone, slate and select materials to validate the home's architectural authenticity. Its discriminating homeowners will never tire of living in a dwelling that is uncompromisingly well-designed and carefully detailed.
Photograph by Danny Piassick

FACING PAGE: We created a Palm Desert home in the exclusive Bighorn Golf Club to perfectly reflect the lifestyle demanded by elite residents. Since outdoor entertaining is the centerpiece of desert living, the regional home needed to possess features that seamlessly meld the interior, exterior, landscape and hardscape. Each facet should feel like an uninterrupted extension of the others. We designed the home to fully maximize the region's ideal climate, extraordinary mountain views and the relaxed, elegant ambience of the prestigious community. Note that the sliding glass wall system removes all boundaries between the home's interior and exterior, making the indoor and outdoor spaces visually one.
Photograph by Lauren Coleman

"Designing a hardscape to look and feel like an extension of the home's interior is imperative; consistent flow creates visual appeal and optimal enjoyment."

—Scott Sangalli

ABOVE: We enjoy working in all architectural genres. Our Prairie-style home exhibits Frank Lloyd Wright influence, designed to suit the homeowner's personal taste. To effectively reach our goals adhering to strict principles of Wright architecture, we had to unify the home and its beautiful setting. We accomplished our mission, and the home exudes timeless appeal. Massing and scale were key considerations, yet great care was given so the home's linear appeal was enhanced, not contradicted, by its natural surroundings. Note that the architecture is complemented and framed by artful landscaping using many native plants, so the property feels like an estate that has always been there.
Photograph by Danny Piassick

FACING PAGE TOP: An outdoor entertaining area was central to this winter retreat for avid golfers. We designed the home's rear hardscape with a curvilinear stone bar that seats eight and is adjacent to a lounging area complete with television and fireplace for the ultimate in alfresco relaxation. What better place for friends to recap golf highlights of the day.
Photograph by Lindsay Marie De Marco

FACING PAGE BOTTOM: Substantial, simple and elegant. You are drawn in as you approach the front door beneath canterra stone arches of the entry tower. Guests step into an open circular courtyard that connects to the main entrance, leading to multiple separate entrances of the guest wing, locker room and casita suite. Good architecture should be a continued invitation: The tower calls you to the courtyard. The courtyard welcomes you to the main entrance. Once inside, the interior extends the invitation through living areas into outdoor surroundings with a covered patio and pool. We believe a well-designed home should capture your attention until you've explored its every element.
Photographs by Lindsay Marie De Marco

POOL-QUEST

Fort Worth, Texas

"Beyond aesthetics, a pool should be designed and crafted without compromise to quality, utility or safety."

—Walter Meek

ABOVE: We designed the pool to appear like a realistic body of water, a tropical paradise with visual and auditory impact. Hand-laid stonework, trickling waterfalls, tropical landscaping and a shallow beach combine to create an oasis in the city. The tight backyard lot and small working environment presented engineering challenges, and we had to carefully consider sloping elevations and drainage issues. Indigenous Texas stone and a deep-toned plaster create a dramatic effect.
Photograph by Steve Edmonds, Star-Telegram

FACING PAGE: For the ultimate elegance, we designed the award-winning swimming pool on multiple elevations to display spilling waterfall features. Tropical landscaping enhances the natural stone deck, and specialty lighting illuminates the pool for a beautiful nightscape. The Tuscan-themed pool with split levels provides refreshing sounds and visual impact. Our timeline was demanding, and sloping elevations, lighting and drainage were important design and construction considerations. The end result: a Mediterranean paradise with island-inspired sights and soothing sounds to enjoy.
Photograph by Walter Meek, Pool-Quest

"Through sophisticated engineering and technology, a well-designed swimming pool integrates sights and sounds for a sensory experience."

—Walter Meek

ABOVE: A backyard pool is more than a place to swim. It is an invitation to escape. Our luxury pool designs consider many factors. How will the pool be used? Are there young children? Is it primarily for exercise or is it a respite at the end of the day? Extraordinary swim-up bars, infinity-edge pool designs that maximize lake views and welcoming hot tubs offer homeowners options for sophisticated poolside entertaining.
Photograph courtesy of Fort Worth Magazine

FACING PAGE: Today's pool experience should offer a fantasy element such as a lagoon-style design or a mountain lake paradise. Water walls offer the ultimate in swimming privacy. Whether contemporary European design or a South Pacific tropical theme, visual and sound elements create an unforgettable experience. We recommend the highest quality materials and excellence in craftsmanship as benchmarks for success when designing a custom pool to last for years to come.
Top left photograph by Walter Meek, Pool-Quest
Top right & bottom photographs by Steve Edmonds, Star-Telegram

index

THE PANACHE COLLECTION

CREATING SPECTACULAR PUBLICATIONS FOR DISCERNING READERS

Dream Homes Series
An Exclusive Showcase of the Finest Architects, Designers and Builders

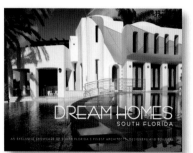

Carolinas
Chicago
Coastal California
Colorado
Deserts
Florida
Georgia
Los Angeles
Metro New York
Michigan
Minnesota
New England
New Jersey

Northern California
Ohio & Pennsylvania
Pacific Northwest
Philadelphia
South Florida
Southwest
Tennessee
Texas
Washington, D.C.

Spectacular Homes Series
An Exclusive Showcase of the Finest Interior Designers

California
Carolinas
Chicago
Colorado
Florida
Georgia
Heartlands
London
Michigan
Minnesota
New England

New York
Ohio & Pennsylvania
Pacific Northwest
Philadelphia
South Florida
Southwest
Tennessee
Texas
Toronto
Washington, D.C.
Western Canada

Perspectives on Design Series
Design Philosophies Expressed by Leading Professionals

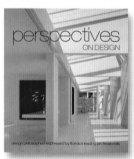

Carolinas
Chicago
Colorado
Florida
Georgia
Minnesota

New England
Pacific Northwest
San Francisco
Southwest

Art of Celebration Series
The Making of a Gala

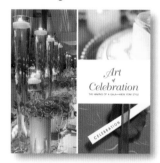

New York
South Florida
Washington, D.C.

Spectacular Wineries Series
A Captivating Tour of Established, Estate and Boutique Wineries

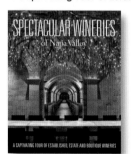

California's Central Coast
Napa Valley
New York
Sonoma County

Specialty Titles
The Finest in Unique Luxury Lifestyle Publications

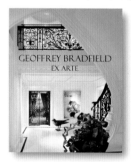

Distinguished Inns of North America
Extraordinary Homes California
Spectacular Golf of Colorado
Spectacular Golf of Texas
Spectacular Hotels
Spectacular Restaurants of Texas
Visions of Design
Geoffrey Bradfield Ex Arte
Cloth and Culture: Couture Creations of Ruth E. Funk
Into the Earth: A Wine Cave Renaissance

City by Design Series
An Architectural Perspective

Atlanta
Charlotte
Chicago
Dallas
Denver
Orlando
Phoenix
San Francisco
Texas

PanacheDesign.com
Where the Design Industry's Finest Professionals Gather, Share and Inspire

PanacheDesign.com overflows with innovative ideas from leading architects, builders, interior designers and other specialists. A gallery of design photographs and library of advice-oriented articles are among the comprehensive site's offerings.

PANACHE PARTNERS, LLC ▪ 1424 GABLES COURT ▪ PLANO, TEXAS 75075 ▪ 469.246.6060 ▪ WWW.PANACHE.COM